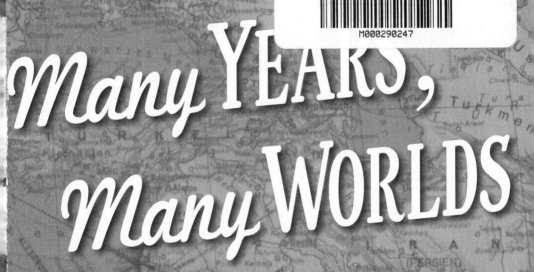

Many YEARS,
Many WORLDS

By BETH H. MACY

This book is dedicated to my mother, whom I loved very much.
Thank you mom, for the gift of your letters.

Chapter One

THE MIDDLE

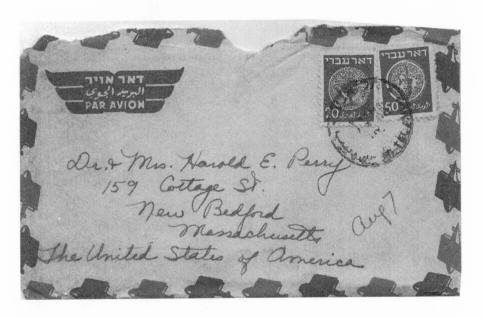

דאר אויר
البريد الجوي
PAR AVION

דאר עברי דאר עברי
20
50

Dr. & Mrs. Harold E. Perry
159 Cottage St.
New Bedford
Massachusetts
The United States of America

Aug 7

15 May 2006

The telephone rang and I jumped at the shrill sound cutting through the expectant silence.

As I listened, my sister informed me: "Mom's kidney values are bad". I heard her relay BUN and Creatine numbers, struggling to understand how bad they were. Should I rush down? My sister handed the phone over to the nurse. The nurse's voice was calm and soothing, "No need to come down here yet. She can go weeks at this rate."

After I hung up I paced around the living room aimlessly. The television was meaningless sound in the background. I finally decided to let out some anxiety by cooking. My great aunt Allie's recipes were all wonderful comfort food – luscious brownies, moist and deeply chocolate, banana bread that was addictive in its subtle flavors and consistency that melted in your mouth, chicken casserole where the golden brown chicken with its buttery flavor mixed sensually with the cream of chicken soup. I decided to cook all three of these favorite recipes – I could always take the extra into work!

As I stood in the kitchen with flour powder scattered all over the counters and floor, I was overwhelmed by this feeling of love and could feel my Allie's presence, so strongly that I started talking to her, telling her what I was cooking.

With a start I realized I was standing in my kitchen talking to my dead great aunt. I ran from the room shaking.

The phone rang again, a burst of sound. My heart was pounding as I answered. It was my sister. She whispered so my mother couldn't hear her, "They tell me that mom's not going to die today but it won't be much longer." I asked to speak to mom and my mother was so happy. I hadn't heard her so happy in such a long time. I was comforted hearing the strength in her voice and told her I'd see her the next day.

I went back into the kitchen and felt Allie's presence again. It was so warm and comforting. I could smell her scent. I hadn't smelled that in years – aromas of kitchen smells, cleaning agents and Lily of the Valley. I closed my eyes. The pain of her loss was too great. I ran again from the kitchen with tears streaming down my face.

I felt unworthy.

16 May 2006 – 3:15 am

I sat up abruptly; awake from a sound sleep. The bedroom was dark and quiet save for the small snores coming from my dog from her bed on the floor beside my bed. I looked over at the digital display on the bedside clock, 3:15am. I said out loud to no one in particular: "My mother just died." Then I thought, "There's nothing I can do about it now." And I fell back into a sound sleep.

16 May 2006 – 6am

My cell phone was ringing downstairs. As I raced down the stairs and grabbed it, the ringing ended. I looked – 4 missed calls from my sister, starting at 3:30 am. I slowly dialed, knowing what I would hear. Mom died shortly after 3am.

It was like a physical blow to hear those words. I felt dizzy, numb as if shot full of Novocain, unable to think. My surroundings had receded as if not part of my current reality. I threw clothing in a bag, not even aware of what I was throwing in.

I don't remember the drive down to the South Shore. The road was a blur through my tears, the trees streams of green along the sides of my vision, my mind full of cotton, my body on autopilot, driving those roads that were so familiar.

---

17 May 2006

I woke up at 3am, tossing and turning, unable to sleep more. I snuck out of the bedroom and sat on the floor of the living room with my computer typing furiously. The glow from the screen was the only light in the room. My mind was racing, words and feelings spilling forth at a rate that my fingers struggled to keep up with. And then I suddenly stopped, spent. I was done for now. I looked at the words on my screen, seemingly foreign as if someone else had typed them, and scrolled down seeing the truth for me.

Yesterday my sister lost her best friend. I lost the most complex relationship I will ever have. I've spent 30 years and thousands of dollars in therapy trying to understand myself, my mother's world, and, my place in relationship to it.

My sister and I shared a childhood with mom but grew up in different worlds. This last year has been a blessing to me because I understand so much more than I ever did.

The mother daughter relationship is stronger than any other. I can't yet grasp fully that she's gone. But both Deb and I know that she will never leave us. And if mom has her way she won't!

I remember looking in the mirror when I was in my 40s and realizing that I had her neck! I was both horrified and delighted. She had a nice neck. I thank her for that but not for the thighs!

My mother and I struggled to understand each other our whole lives. We were so alike in some ways and had such fundamental differences in others. She liked everything male and I liked everything female. Our worlds were so foreign to each other. I remember her picking up the shrink-wrapped Symphony computer software box that I so proudly brought home and saying - "You made this dear? And people use it on a computer?" Shortly afterwards she took a computer course! I think it was both out of a desire to understand better what I did and to not be bested at something.

In all of that she loved me deeply and I her. She was a strong woman with a will of steel. She hung on my desk the saying: "Tender Hearted touch a nettle it will sting you or your pains. But grasp it like a man of mettle and it soft as silk remains."

We butted heads from the day I could talk and tantrum. She was fierce and creative. My sister and I remember her dragging us around the house by our hair and faking a heart attack for us to behave. Mom once told me she wanted two little baby girls who would be a reflection of her. I think that in some way I disappointed her.

My mother was a brilliant woman. Her mind was always working. Even in her last year she was designing houses in her head to keep alert. I know she was very frustrated her last day as she struggled to spell the word coffee on a shopping list for my sister. Her mind had always been there for her and I think it was the last straw for her as it too failed.

My mother was an accomplished artist. Her watercolors were masterful. I grew up with watercolor paper soaking in the bathtub and sections of the Famous Artist Course scattered around the house. She made beautiful ceramic dolls that I could admire even though I couldn't relate to them. It was the fine dust from the doll making as well as many years of cigarette smoking that wrecked her lungs. In later years she turned to oil paints. But watercolor was her legacy to the world. She controlled a wash like no other!

Mom loved music. I grew up with a love for Aida and South Pacific because of her constant playing of it. She was an original Beatle's fan and took my sister and me to see them in NY. We all would sing a lot. In recent years she had three CD players in her three-room house. When she could no longer drive she would sit in her car and listen to music in the driveway. Then back the car up and down just to prove that she could still do that!

She hated to drive but loved her cars. We had an old Desoto growing up that she liked but it was the white Impala that she adored. She always wanted a little red sports car. I think her last car, although white, came the closest to that dream car for her. It was very hard for her to give that up.

This past year Debbie and I were ripping up her old linoleum floor and singing old songs from our childhood. She was listening to us and remarked how depressed she was when we were growing up. It brought a lot of things into perspective for me, especially when I was searching through Old Della Reese songs to find one to play for her funeral and listening to the words.

She taught me to splice wires together and helped me build my own bedroom at 85 Armour St, cleverly carving a plywood-and-2x4 structure out of the dining room. From her I got my love of art stores and hardware stores.

She was a physical woman. She was always dragging my sister and me out for long walks or bike-rides or tennis games. She was so frustrated not being able to do things any more. One of her caretakers told me how delighted she was her last week when she walked a few steps (aided) to the bathroom. Her love of exercise is one that I have shared with many people through my exercise programs. I have quoted her many times. I have engraved in my memory her saying of why sit when you can stand, why stand when you can walk, why walk when you can run.

My mother loved clothes. She loved to shop. One of her happiest days this past year was when my sister took her in a wheelchair to Filenes. She marveled at all the colors and delighted in her bargains.

My mother was a fierce lioness who protected her territory. She loved my sister and my sister's children deeply and defended them fiercely. She was a Leo to the core. She was proud, vain and loved to be admired.

She loved nature although I never realized how much until a day around 10 years ago when she and I were walking in Buttonwood Park and we saw this beautiful gnarly old tree and both had to go touch it and admire it. It was a rare and wonderful bonding experience. She loved birds and it was so sad when she could no longer hear them sing. Her expression for happiness was always hearing the birds sing inside.

My mother had a deep belief in God but did not like much of organized religion. But she loved the comfort of going to church. It brought to her the structure and memories of her childhood. And she loved the poetry of the scripture. I remember her home schooling us in the bible with her drawings of Moses and the rushes. I'm afraid I have her to thank for my non-traditional view of religion. I know, as she grew older, it brought her more and more comfort to think that she would be finally with her father (both God and her real father). She missed her father, mother, and Allie very much. I know she is with them now.

My mother was very angry with her father, but would never admit it. It surprised her when she saw a glimpse of these feelings in her 60's. One *day we were talking about dogs and she was saying how much my golden retriever, Margo reminded her of her beloved cocker spaniel. When she was away with Dad, her dog barked too much so her father put it to sleep. She shook her fist at the air and cursed him for doing that. I hope she's finally able to tell him how she feels.*

My mother was afraid of much of life. Travel frightened her. Even long drives in the car. She traveled halfway around the world with my father and then stayed the rest of her life in her comfort zone of New Bedford. After my own trip to India I was amazed that she could have done such a trip especially at a time when the world was "bigger" and "more foreign". She was the only white woman in many situations. I asked her "Mom, weren't you afraid?" She thought a bit and said, "No dear, I was with your father."

But there were other parts of life that she embraced with a passion, flouting conventions. My mother was an earthy woman. She was the original Mrs. Robinson and enjoyed the many aspects of the late 60's and 70's that many of us fondly recollect as college students. She was unconventional in many ways. She created and lived in her own world and kept much of the harsh reality outside of that world at bay. As a child she would build a magical invisible cocoon around us to guard us from the rest of the world. She would be horrified at me talking about less than a perfect picture of her.

My mother claimed to be a people person but hated crowds and parties. I remember one party at my house where she sat in the back room with my nephew watching TV. She had helped me prepare the dishes for that party and put a special swirl on the dip. I was so amazed that she knew how to do that. She told me that her parents had always thrown parties when she was growing up. It didn't sound like she liked those parties much.

My mother had an excellent sense of humor. On her last day on earth she was telling little jokes and laughing. She was very happy. I think she knew she was finally going home.

My mother always was sympathetic when you were sick. I remember the cambric tea and toast that she would bring me when I wasn't feeling well as a child. I think that being sick was when she got attention from her father.

There is a huge hole inside of me, and great pain. And I know it's even worse for Deb. But we all did our best. It may have fallen short of our expectations at times, but we did our best. And that is all anyone can ever do. Mom did her best. She had limited tools at her disposal. She was a woman of many parts. But she brought a color to life, a fierce will, and a passion. It was always confusing to see her hide and run when she had all that. But I embraced those concepts. I grew up a reaction to her and an embodiment of what she preached. I have so much to thank her for. I know she knows that.

Mom was the one person that, even when she wasn't talking to me, always cared. And when she was, was always there on the other end of the phone. I will miss her so much.

7 am

I sat staring at the words on the computer screen, feeling so empty - a hollow feeling inside, that nothing could fill.

17 May 2006

The wake…

As I walked through the massive doorway into the funeral home, I was struck by the decayed grandeur, the faded oriental rugs, the musty smell covered by the pungent scent of flowers, the silence, the lack of life. I stood before mom's casket, my mind struggling to reconcile her being alive just a few days before, and now, in that blue box. It seemed too small to hold her.

I paced around looking at the picture of her in her 20's, the cards, the flowers, feeling the concern and love from each of my friends. I didn't want to be there. It was the final step in being a grown-up. There was no-one left to buffer me. No one older and wiser was there to comfort me.

I stood in the back of the room as people arrived. A blur of faces, murmuring voices, halting bits of conversation swirling around, a maze of confusion. Nothing real. It couldn't be real. If I felt the reality, I would just break down. I looked for familiar faces to focus on, glancing at my watch, praying for the time to be over. There was still the funeral to go through. I wanted to run away.

---

18 May 2006

The funeral...

The day dawned bright and clear. It was a day that mom would have loved. It was a fitting day for a final farewell.

Again I made the trip to the funeral home. This time when I arrived it was full of people standing awkwardly, unsure of what to say, murmuring platitudes. The minister was old and feeble. He had known mom many years, but couldn't remember her name. His sermon left me wondering whom he was talking about. I felt angry – she deserved more – she deserved someone to tell this audience who she was.

I stood up and faced the room. I took the folded pieces of paper from my pocket and slowly unfolded them. My hands were shaking and my voice quivered as I started reading: "Yesterday my sister lost her best friend. I lost the most complex relationship I will ever have…" Again the blur of faces as I made my way to my car, feeling so lost. I distantly heard clapping when I finished. I stood feeling lost, empty and drained, and then was ushered to my car by the funeral director.

The drive to the cemetery behind the hearse was the longest I have ever done. The slow pace was excruciating. We weaved our way through the narrow streets, stopping at stop sign after stop sign. A long parade of cars all held together by an invisible string. I could hardly hold onto the steering wheel I was shaking so hard. Tears streamed down my face again. The steering wheel felt foreign under my hands. I didn't feel connected to my hands or feet. All I knew was that I was following my mother to her final resting place. "Do you want me to drive?" "No, this is something I have to do."

I felt my brother in law's hand steadying me on one side, my partner's on the other. I could hardly stand. They had the casket positioned over the hole. I didn't hear what the minister was saying. I couldn't stop crying.

"We will lower her down once you have left." I thought of the Jewish tradition of shoveling dirt in and thought how much completeness that gives you rather than walking away. I didn't want to leave.

My sister suggested, "Let's go find Grandpa's grave." "Where is it?" We left as a pack, invisibly supporting each other, wandering through the cemetery without a clue where we were heading. It just felt good to walk. We failed miserably to find the other grave and laughed about that. We were restored enough to return to the grave.

Mom's blue casket was lowered in. I took a yellow rose and threw it in on top of the casket. It made a satisfying thump of finality.

---

23 May 2006

"She didn't talk a lot about her past. I wish I had learned more. "

I grabbed a Kleenex out of the box next to me on the couch and blew my nose. My therapist looked at me expectantly. I knew she was going to ask how I felt about it, so I reached inside myself for more.

"I just feel sad, very sad, ..."

The room was filled with silence... The pain was too much to talk further. I looked around her office for a distraction. My eyes struggled through the blur of the tears to read titles on the books in her bookshelf. I looked down at my hands and tried to recognize them as mine.

"I miss her so much."

Again the tears spilled forth. I had spent the past year crying as her health failed and now the tears just kept coming. I was so sick of crying. I wanted happiness.

"Our relationship was so complex. I know she loved me. But I think in the end she was sick of me."

I hugged a stuffed animal and rocked back and forth for a while as I cried.

"When I looked at her filmy, pale blue, cataract covered eyes as she sat there in the nursing home, I was so looking for a trace of the mother I knew, for a connection to her. I couldn't find it. I would sit there and wonder why I came down to see her. It seemed so stilted and painful for both of us. The one time we laughed was when I tried to get her from her wheelchair to the bed and had to swing her around and sit down with her on top of me. She was 90 pounds of dead weight! She laughed so hard. And I did too. I felt so inadequate though."

I looked again for a distraction and remembered an article I had found on the web. I took a crumpled piece of paper from my pocket and handed it to my therapist.

"I've been trying to find pieces of her past, to understand who she was. Perhaps by that I can know more who we were?"

Chapter Two

AN EARLIER TIME...

War-scarred street
in Jerusalem.

November 8, 1949

Start of Operation Magic Carpet

The primary goal of the State of Israel is to be the safe homeland of all Jews. This was best portrayed in its secret national projects to bring distressed Jewish communities "home" to Israel.[1]

Finally, nearly 50,000 traditionally religious Yemeni Jews, who had never seen a plane, were airlifted to Israel in 1949 and in 1950 in Operation "Magic Carpet." Since the Book of Isaiah promised, "They shall mount up with wings, as eagles". The Jewish community boarded "The Eagles" contentedly; to the pilots consternation some of them lit a bonfire aboard, to cook their food.[2]

23 May 2006

"I've been rummaging through everything trying to hold on to pieces of her: my memory, the web, books, her house.... I just feel such an empty hole inside of me. I remember her saying that they flew the Jews over Arab territory into the newly found state of Israel. She mentioned them bringing goats onboard, and lighting fires on the cabin floor, and losing an engine over Arab territory and nearly being shot down. I wish I had asked more questions. I have been looking for more information. I found that snippet on the web."

1   http://www.wzo.org.il/en/resources/view.asp?id=1062&flag=true

2   http://www.hsje.org/Jews%20Kicked%20out%20
    of%20Arab%20Lands%20Part%202.htm

I was talking really quickly now, trying to fill up the emptiness inside of me and to avoid looking further into it.

"I also found a clipping of a 1973 New Bedford Standard Times obituary in a book she had read. You know one of those romance novels? A Nora Roberts, I think. It was about some guy called David Ben-Gurion. It had some importance to her. I would have loved to know why. I threw it out. There was just too much paper to wade through. I wish I had kept it now."

"OK, enough for today. 10 minutes left? I don't think I have anything left to say."

"How do I feel?"

"Sigh…"

I felt like I had been run over by a truck and stopped dead in my tracks. I didn't know what to do next.

"Lost. Lost and confused."

I didn't want to leave the office. I grabbed one more piece of paper from my pocket and thrust it at my therapist.

"I have this letter I found too."

May 26th (1949?)

Dear Folks,

Tel-Aviv, sewers flooding streets and sidewalk, noise, dirt, flies, stomach trouble: - all these are synonymous to me. Which is the reason I must mail my letters elsewhere, for the censors would never permit such reports of the Promised Land to reach the States. Which is also why I shall be very glad to clear out of here, as we're planning on or around the 10th of June. McGuire is due in with the 54th today & may be able to give us an idea of how long the 46 will be operating around Hong Kong. There's now an austerity program on in Tel-Aviv, & while it does cut down on the price of a meal, it also cuts

down considerably the amount of the meal.
Last night Herb & I followed dinner at one restaurant with dinner at another!

A couple more trips to Asmara are scheduled
before we leave. If the 46 gets back from Djiborti
tonight, tomorrow Herb is taking me to Asmara
& leaving me there until he comes on the next
trip. Then I'll have a chance to get some decent
food & build up resistance to combat the "Hong
Kong Blues" - which they say everyone has a
bat with when first going there. Some fun! It
will be nice to see the Cutbushes, Mrs. Saruppi,
Patti Gilmore & the rest of our friends there. I
do wish we could have been stationed

---

23 May 2006

"That's the end of the letter – I can't find page two. She had
so many things just mixed in together – drawers full of junk and

clothing and then wonderful finds like this letter. I'm still sorting things out"

I looked at the clock across the room and knew we were running out of time. The hands on the clock sometimes moved at a glacial pace but now were racing to the finish of our hour. I distractedly answered my therapist's question. So much was crowded into my head that I thought it would burst. The pain in my chest was so intense it seemed real.

"Yes, that sorting things out phrase does have many levels of meaning...of course! I never really knew my mom. We were so very different. We struggled all our lives to understand each other. I'm still searching and trying to understand her. She was so much. And so little."

I knew time was up and looked for somewhere to throw away my wadded up pieces of Kleenex.

"It's nice that you have so many boxes of Kleenex around, but you need more wastebaskets near the couch. Oh thanks..."

"It's time already? Yes, I will continue to do writing."

I reluctantly left that place of comfort and support.

---

24 May 2006 -3:15am

Mom – Why did you leave?!

Come Back!!!

Damn it.

25 May 2006

I walked into my therapist's office and struggled to see my surroundings. I felt trapped inside my head and the swirl of my emotions. I tried to focus on her face and connect to reality.

"I cry every day. It's so hard to be around people and pretend
to function."

Tears streamed down my face. My mind was blanked from being
so full.

"I need a Kleenex."

I reached out my hand and took the box that was offered. Part
of my mind registered that it was a blue rectangular box.

"Thanks…"

I drew my knees up and hugged them as I cried. I blew my nose
again and again hoping I'd stop crying. I struggled through the
fog in my head for something to say.

"I am so sick of blowing my nose and being congested. All I want
to do is sort through the stuff from her house. It makes me feel
like there's still a connection."

I was shaking and sick to my stomach from crying so much. And
I was so sick of crying.

"This Kleenex box is empty."

Again as I reached for the box I noticed it was a different color
and square. I laughed.

"A new box, thanks. Just put it on my bill."

I was glad to smile and found the mist clearing a bit, enough
that a calm came in. I would be ok for a while. I tried to answer her

look of concern. I started speaking very quickly again. 'Show and Tell' to avoid the emotions.

"There's so much to sort through. I don't know what I'm searching for."

"I found this scrap of paper:"

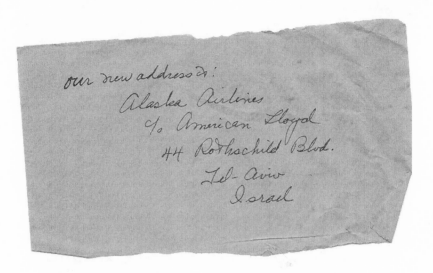

"It's mom's handwriting...so familiar. I look at it and get a pang of sorrow that settles into a solid feeling in my chest and a heavy feeling around my eyes."

I moved on quickly before the tears could come again...

"I also found this letter:"

8 June 1949

June 8th

YARDEN HOTEL/130, BEN-YEHUDA St.,
TEL-AVIV / PHONE 3732

Dear Folks,

There's been no particular news of late. We got a cable that Wooten is on his way here via Hong Kong. Tomorrow we're going to Haifa to get our visas for India & Hong Kong - transient visas for Pakistan & India - & will leave as soon as we get them,, regardless of whether or not Wooten has arrived. Looks like there'll be more business in this area if he's coming.

F.D.R., Jr. is in Tel-Aviv at present, & this noon we're lunching at the Katie-Dan where he's staying on chance we may see him.

In Asmara we had tea with a Mrs. Haft - friend of Mr. Simon's - & dinner at the Ahronni's. It was an eight-course meal - each course a feed in itself, & at 10 o'clock at night at that! We were all thoroughly stuffed by the time we left Asmara. We also visited two nightclubs there, & dancing at that altitude really gets you. It's nice to be back in Tel-Aviv where you can take a deep breath without your heart racing & getting short-winded!

Did a big washing & ironing yesterday - 2 shirts, 3 dresses, my white suit, plus underwear. It would have cost over twelve American dollars *to have that much laundry done out here! Went to the beach in the afternoon, but the surf was too high to swim, so spent a quiet time reading & knitting at home & danced downstairs here at the hotel in the evening.*

This morning we had an eight o'clock appointment for breakfast with a man from American Lloyd[3].

The weather has been beautiful & sunny here - it is a lovely climate. No news from home for ages. I'll find out the name of Alaska's agent in Hong Kong so that you can write us c/o them till we get an address.

Loads of love,

Tinky X

---

3   According to www.americanlloyd.com: "American Lloyd Travel Services, established in 1933, is a leading corporate and leisure travel agency in Singapore, and is part of the Sampoerna Group of Companies."

25 May 2006

"I wish I had listened more in history class. I had to look up
F.D.R. Jr.![4] This is what I found." I handed my therapist a wrinkled
printout.

Franklin Delano Roosevelt, Jr.
From Wikipedia, the free encyclopedia

Franklin Delano Roosevelt, Jr. (August 17, 1914 – August 17, 1988)
was the fifth child of Anna Eleanor Roosevelt and Franklin D. Roosevelt
(the 32nd President of the United States). He was born at his parents'
summer home at Campobello Island, New Brunswick, Canada – now a
historic site. An earlier child of the same name died in infancy.
    He was a Naval officer in World War II and was decorated for bravery
in the battle of Casablanca.
    He graduated from Harvard University in 1937, and the University
of Virginia Law School on June 10, 1940. During his graduation, his
father, Franklin D. Roosevelt gave what is known as the "Stab in the Back"
Speech, criticizing Italy's entry into the war.
    Roosevelt, who was often referred to as "FDR Jr.", served as a member
of the United States Congress, representing the Twentieth District of New
York from 1949 to 1954. In 1949 he won a special election running
as a candidate of the Liberal Party of New York, although he later
ran on the Democratic ticket as well. Roosevelt unsuccessfully sought
the Democratic nomination for Governor in 1954, but was chosen by

---

4   http://en.wikipedia.org/wiki/Franklin_Delano_Roosevelt,_Jr.

the Democratic State Convention (New York State did not have pri-
maries for statewide office until 1968) as the Democratic candidate
for Attorney-General. Roosevelt was defeated in the general election by
Republican Jacob Javits.

He campaigned for John F. Kennedy in the 1960 West Virginia primary,
and Kennedy later named him Under-Secretary of Commerce and chair-
man of the President's Appalachian Regional Commission.

He unsuccessfully ran for Governor of New York as a Tammany Hall
candidate affiliated with the Liberal Party in 1966.

He served as chairman of the Equal Employment Opportunity
Commission May 26, 1965 - May 11, 1966.

He was senior partner in the New York law firm of Roosevelt and Freiden
before and after his service in the Congress.

He had five marriages, including one to Ethel du Pont of the du Pont
family of industrialists. Their marriage produced two sons, Franklin
Delano Roosevelt, III (b. 1938) and Christopher du Pont Roosevelt (b.
1941). The couple separated and formally divorced in 1949. In total, he
had 5 children from his several marriages.

He also ran a small cattle farm, and imported Fiat automobiles.

Franklin Delano Roosevelt, Jr. died in Poughkeepsie, New York after a
battle with lung cancer, on his 74th birthday, August 17, 1988.

"I wonder what on earth he was doing in Tel-Aviv?"

I knew my therapist didn't want to hear about FDR, Jr. and that
I was paying to get me back in shape but still I struggled to find
something to say next that wouldn't make me feel and cry.

"Mom sounded happy in Tel-Aviv – she liked the climate & the
altitude... It sounds like she enjoyed dancing too, and that she

and Dad were having fun too. I don't know if she ever danced late in life. She was always active."

I remembered her dragging us out on bike-rides all over the city and out into the countryside. I looked again for something unrelated to my true feelings. I was so drained from crying.

"I didn't know she could knit, but she was a wonderful seamstress. She made all the clothes for her porcelain dolls as well as for these clothespin dolls she made us to play with as kids. We had the Beatles, complete with jackets that came off, and a Dad doll, and a Heather doll, Deb's doll, "Mushie", used to careen through town in her wooden car and crash into trees and houses. Mom made the entire town out of cardboard boxes. Her house had lights in it from a Xmas tree strand that she wired within the walls of the cardboard house. She was very creative."

I paused as memories flowed through my head of those cardboard houses scattered around the bedroom, dust bunnies under the bed, centipedes running by, such creativity with so little. My mind felt split, one part trapped in the past, the other trying to live the present.

"I'm not sure who the other people are. I wonder if she ever kept in touch with them. She seemed not to have any friends when we were growing up. I can't remember her going out at all."

"Breathe?"

I stopped and looked around the room. Sunlight was streaming in the window. I was clutching a pillow from the couch. I slowly put it back where it belonged. I heard my therapist's voice as if through a fog.

"Time's up? OK see you next week. Thanks."

30 May 2006

I walked into my therapist's office, took off my shoes and sat on the couch, hugging my knees, with my feet up in front of me. My head hurt, my face felt drawn, I had a solid ache in my chest. I looked around the office uncertain where to begin. Then I remembered I had brought another show and tell piece.

"I found this information on the Alaska Airlines web site and printed it out:"[5]

When Alaska Airlines sent them on "Operation Magic Carpet" 50 years ago, Warren and Marian Metzger didn't realize they were embarking on an adventure of a lifetime.

Warren, a DC-4 captain, and Marian, a flight attendant, were part of what turned out to be one of the greatest feats in Alaska Airlines' 67-year history: airlifting thousands of Yemenite Jews to the newly created nation of Israel.

The logistics of it all made the task daunting. Fuel was hard to come by. Flight and maintenance crews had to be positioned through the Middle East. And the desert sand wreaked havoc on engines.

It took a whole lot of resourcefulness the better part of 1949 to do it. But in the end, despite being shot at and even bombed upon, the mission was accomplished – and without a single loss of life.

Known as the lost tribe of Israel, the Yemenite Jews had wandered the deserts for at least two centuries after being driven out of Palestine. Nomads, they had never seen an airplane and never lived anywhere but a tent.

---

5   http://www.alaskaair.com/www2/company/History/MagicCarpet.asp

Ironically, their faith included a prophecy that they would be returned to their Holy Land on the wings of eagles.

"One of the things that really got to me was when we were unloading a plane at Tel Aviv," said Marian, who assisted Israeli nurses on a number of flights. "A little old lady came up to me and took the hem of my jacket and kissed it. She was giving me a blessing for getting them home. We were the wings of eagles."

For both Marian and Warren, the assignment came on the heels of flying the airline's other great adventure of the late 1940s: the Berlin Airlift.

"I had no idea what I was getting into, absolutely none," remembered Warren, who retired in 1979 as Alaska's chief pilot and vice president of flight operations. "It was pretty much seat-of-the-pants flying in those days. Navigation was by dead reckoning and eyesight. Planes were getting shot at. The airport in Tel Aviv was getting bombed all the time. We had to put extra fuel tanks in the planes so we had the range to avoid landing in Arab territory."

British officials advised them that Arabs, angry over the establishment of the Jewish state, would certainly kill all the passengers and likely the whole crew if they were forced to land on Arab soil. Many planes were shot at.

Days often lasted between 16 and 20 hours and the one-way flights, in twin-engine C-46 or DC-4 aircraft, covered nearly 3,000 miles.

"We'd take off from our base in Asmara (in Eritrea) in the morning and fly to Aden (in Yemen) to pick up our passengers and refuel," Warren said. "Then we'd fly up the Red Sea and the Gulf of Aqaba to the airport at Tel Aviv to unload. Then we'd fly to Cyprus for the night. We couldn't keep the planes on the ground in Israel because of the bombings."

"One of our pilots got a little bit too close to Arab territory when flying into Israel from the Gulf of Aqaba and tracers started arching up toward

the plane," Warren said. "Another one of our planes got a tire blown out during a bombing raid in Tel Aviv. One of our crews practically lived on their plane from the end of April through June."

Bob Maguire, another Alaska pilot, once had to drop down to several hundred feet above the ground, squirming through hills and passes, to evade Arab gunfire.

What Warren and Marian thought was a temporary assignment turned into a seven-month mission of mercy. It also launched a marriage that has also celebrated its golden anniversary. Warren and Marian were married in Asmara in January 1949.

"I had met Warren when I started working for Alaska in July of 1948," Marian said. "We had both worked the Berlin airlift. I was sent to Shanghai and I didn't know where Warren was. I landed in Asmara after one flight and when the door of the plane opened, one of the guys who knew I'd been seeing Warren from time to time said he was in Tel Aviv and he'd be flying in the next day."

Before her Operation Magic Carpet flights in the Middle East, Marian, who retired from Alaska in 1952, assisted on flights from Shanghai transporting Jews who fled to China to escape persecution in Germany. When communists came to power in China, the German Jews took flight again to Israel.

"We had been doing a lot of trips, a lot of different kinds of trips," Marian said. "We realized this was going to be part of the history of Israel, but it seemed like more of an adventure at the time."

In all, with the help of Alaska Airlines, charter carriers and the military, more than 40,000 Yemenite Jews were airlifted to Israel between late 1948 and early 1950.

30 May 2006

"See it mentions Bob Maguire! I wrote them to see if I could find out more! There's very little on the web that I can find. My stepmom said that Leon Uris based one of his pilots in the Exodus on Dad. I always meant to write him and find out if he knew him. But now it's too late. He's dead too."

My chest felt tight. I found it hard to breathe. I reached for another Kleenex. As if in the distance I heard my therapist ask what I was feeling.

"Of course I feel sad! Angry? Well yes, a bit. Why didn't she tell us more? I know she was so angry herself... I'm also angry that this Warren and Marion got written up and not my parents."

I looked across the room. The clock hands were on the hour. I felt jumbled inside. I stood up to leave. I felt unsteady on my feet. I looked at my shoes as if they were foreign objects.

"Yes I'll do some writing when I get home. I'll see you Thursday."

I squared my shoulders and walked to the door, the room out of focus, my head trapped in the past.

19 June 1949 - Bombay

Sunday June 19ᵗʰ

Dear Folks,

We got into the airport here early Friday evening. Ted, Ford & Reis were put in quarantine when we passed through the health department. They'd had their shots pre-dated by the Asmara doctor as of 10 days ago, but it seems that Asmara is in a yellow fever zone & requires 15 days for immunity. So the poor fellows were marched off to the hospital while Blackie, Herb & I came out to the West End hotel. When we made our trip to Haifa, the American consul there told us we didn't need visas for Bombay. Now we find we do, so Blackie spent yesterday morning running around to straighten that out, as a result of which we were all invited to the American Vice Consul's apartment for a social chat at 9 last night. He's a young fellow, & afterwards he drove us around Bombay. We went up on a hill & looked over the city & its lights, drove through the better residential district with its huge, oriental-looking houses, and then down to a district called "The Cages" - where both sides of the street for several blocks there are cages of prostitutes, posing & preening in doorways to attract business. The smells of Bombay are pungent to say the least. We had a regular Indian meal here at the hotel - with curried lamb & everything so highly spiced you have to drink a quart of water with it.

Yesterday afternoon Herb & I went shopping in the native bazaars to get some white bucks &

shirt for him & also got two beautiful saris for me. They're a very fine nylon with hand embroidery - one soft pink with a deep border embroidered in silver, & the other a heavenly blue, embroidered with gold & a touch of crimson. There's enough in each to make an evening gown, & last night Herb & I were draping them on me & trying them differ- ent ways. Today we're going to visit the "Hanging Gardens" - where they have beautiful flowering shrubs & shrubs cut in shape of animals. The boys get out of hock this noon & tomorrow morning we'll be on our way. It's been a nice break to the trip stopping here.

Loads & loads of love to all,

X Tinky X

1 June 2006

I walked into my therapist's office and sat immediately on the couch and started talking. There was so much inside I thought I would burst.

"I didn't think mom liked blue. Last year I bought her blue sneakers and she asked me to return them. She loved her little pink slippers and sneakers I bought her though. She claimed she liked the purple ones too but I never saw her in anything but the pink ones. I tried to get her a pink coffin but they only had blue. I felt guilty about that, but also, in a way, happy that I was burying her in a color she didn't like. I resented having to pay for her funeral. I resented being the person with the money, only wanted for my money. Well she didn't hate blue at least...it just wasn't her favorite color. You know she didn't like chocolate either? How could someone not like chocolate? Ok – I'm breathing..."

I felt hollow. I looked for something to hold on to and pulled the pillow to my chest.

"Please pass the Kleenex...thanks. Yes, I do feel like a bad person. I resented that I had to support her. That I paid for the roof over her head."

Memories of mom walking around the yard with her pink sneakers on flowed through my head: a snippet of her walking slowly across the lawn, looking frail and unsteady, a confused look on her face.

I looked down at the letter in my hands.

"She would be in heaven though being draped in nice cloth and getting all that attention! It does sound like mom and Dad had fun together."

More vignettes: Mom wandering back towards the house, a sandwich with only a bit taken out of it on her plate by her chair, the dappled light filtered by the maple tree, the pink sneakers doing their magic of holding her up...

"I do remember her talking about the street with prosti-tutes. That made a big impression on her! I can't imagine her walking down that street. She was much more cosmopolitan than I ever imagined! But I would have loved to have seen the expression on her face! I'm sure she'd never seen anything like that before!"

My head had a vision of mom in the kitchen when I was young, her hair pinned up on top of her head, whispers of it streaming down around her face, her eyes looking tired and her face gaunt. I talked faster to cover the vision. My chest hurt again.

"I've been doing some research to see what life was like in the States during the 1940's and found some great info:"

"Look at this style: [6]"

---

6   http://www.angelfire.com/retro2/lisanostalgia1/40s.html

the "New Look"
The end of the war meant the end
of fabric rationing. In 1947,
Christian Dior's *New Look* brought us out of
our fashion doldrums with full skirts and
ultra-feminine frills.

I remembered mom's long skirts that I could hide behind when I was young. Her wearing gloves to church, and hats, her love of Christian Dior fashions and Chanel Number 5 perfume. I pulled out another scrap of paper and passed it across to my therapist to distract my mind and her questions.

"I also found some information about being a debutant on this web site:"

debutantes

The tradition of making your *debut* in adult society came from England, and gained popularity in America in the late 1800's. Upper-class girls of marrying age "came out" at parties and debutante balls...this was a formal announcement that she was eligible for marriage to suitable young men. In this way, young ladies were guided into the proper social circles, and well-to-do families could maintain (or raise) their social standing.

In the 40's, debutantes often performed charity work or took on special projects. In 1947, the "Deb Of The Year" was none other than Jacqueline Bouvier Kennedy Onassis. The classic "debutante look" consisted of light-colored evening gowns and above-the-elbow white gloves. Debutante Registers were published each year, featuring photos and details about the young ladies.

debs of the 40's
Oona O'Neill
Valerie Axtell
Jacqueline Bouvier
Gloria Vanderbilt

"Looks like my mom was in good company there! She was fasci-nated by stories of Jackie Kennedy. I think she had the same sense of style and class as Jackie did. Perhaps it was the era."

A vision of mom's old grey Desoto with it's rounded lines popped into my head. I so loved that car and loved riding in it with mom. I talked faster.

"Although I don't think the war touched the United States in the same way it did overseas, the years after the war must have been ones of such freedom, possibility and expansion. A bit self-indulgent perhaps? We have lost so much by not capturing the oral history of that generation."

A wave of regret washed over me. I lost so many opportunities to talk to my mother. My surroundings were blurred and distant. I touched the fabric of the couch and felt its smoothness.

"And yes, we've lost so much in losing that generation. Yes, I've lost a lot – both parents had such rich histories and backgrounds."

I had a vision of mom smoking a cigarette, the red of her lipstick on the filter, the smoke swirling around her head…her showing me how to blow smoke rings…me entranced by her.

"Funny, growing up you always think that you know so much more than your parents and that they couldn't understand what you're going through…."

I heard my mom's voice echoing in my head, plaintively asking, "Where did we go wrong? What happened to our relationship?"

"It's a hard realization finally being an adult…"

I felt dizzy from the waves of pain flowing through me, coming out my eyes.

"Yes, I do need the Kleenex."

My mind raced, pictures and feelings overwhelming me with the speed at which they raced through. I grasped at snippets rushing by:

"Why couldn't I have gotten to this point without losing mom?"

"Life sucks..."

"No I don't mean that..."

"It's such a process..."

"I want both my mom back...and my dad ...I miss them both."

I struggled to get grounded. Looked at the plant growing down the bookcase. Mom had a green ivy like that.

"OK – next week it is..."

---

3 June 2007

I could feel the cold of the earth seeping through the knees of my slacks as I knelt in the dirt, tears streaming down my face as I clawed the grass up from around the rose bush I had just planted. I said softly, "Here mom, this is for you." My mother always loved roses.

A cardinal landed on the tree above the spot where I knelt, chirping rhythmically. I blew my nose and then whistled in reply. He whistled back. I wiped the tears from my face feeling the grit from my fingers mix in and smear on my cheeks. I whistled back at the bird thinking how perfect this was for mom: birds and roses – she so loved both. I started bawling again, doubled up on my knees in my front yard, holding myself tight to keep from exploding in pain.

6 June 2006

I entered the therapist's office and sat down and felt angry with myself. I knew I was just going to barrel ahead with show and tell again.

"I found a bunch of letters in the old shed. She had just shoved them in an old garbage bag box!"

I couldn't stop myself. I somehow needed to work through my pain in this way. But I was angry that I took so long to get at what I was feeling and instead was showing a garbage bag box off!

"Amazing that they didn't get ruined from the weather. She wanted them but apparently didn't want them in the house. And shoving them in a garbage bag box is rather telling of how she felt, hey?"

I took a breath. I felt such anger at mom. My forehead hurt from frowning. My eyes darted about the room to find something happy. I saw the box of crayons and smiled. A memory of opening up a box of Crayola crayons and smelling that unique waxy smell and seeing that beautiful rainbow of colors and possibilities open up before me.

"They're not in any sort of order. Some don't even seem to be in their correct envelopes. I want to read them slowly. Just take one at a time as it is in the box and see what it tells me."

Undated – sometime in 1949

& showed me where to get pasteurized milk - the first I'd had since leaving the States & did that glass of milk taste good! We had a wedding dinner at night - courtesy of the Maguires - & then all went to bed early and locked our doors. But pretty soon there was a knock - Blackie was lonesome! So he came in

and sat on the bed to talk - & then Ted came around, too! What a funny life.

It's confusing to get used to the ~~chan~~ change from East African rupees & shillings to the Palestine mils & piastros - I'm not sure of the spelling, but that's how it's pronounced! Now for a nap & to bed early tonight to try & knock this blooming cold out of me before Herb gets back - so we won't keep passing it on to each other.

Cont'd Sunday aft: -

They came in to move us to a room of our own, as I was writing this yesterday. I spent all evening getting things put away & now we have a nice room decorated in blue & with adjourning shower. I feel much more as if we'd really set up housekeeping at last. This morning I tackled

all our dirty laundry - which was consider-
able since I had no chance to do any before.
Now Herb's shirts & my slips, etc. are drying
on racks on the balcony outside the Maguire's
room. As they get damp-dry, I bring them in
& iron them with the iron we got in Aden and
on a new ironing & sleeve board I bought here
this morning. The shirts will have to go without
starching - it costs about one dollar to have
them laundered out. It looks as if I've been
taking in washing - you should see the pile!

Right now I'm sitting in the sun on our
balcony - our room is right below the Maguires' -
& drinking a cup of Nescafe, for which I heated
the water on our electric kettle - having swiped
a plug from one of the hotel lamps. It' wonderful to feel we have a home here, & I'm anxious
for Herb to see it when he gets back tonight. It's

not bad when he's away for just a short trip like this - & all this washing & ironing keeps me too busy to be too lonesome. Yesterday it looked like my cold was really going to keep me up a while, but I started on the Sulfamirazine & that's done wonders - thank goodness!

Now to go on with my ironing. I feel quite domestic & very happy that Herb will be back tonight. He's a very nice husband & I kind of miss not having him around!

Loads of love to all - including Burpie, Widgie, & my Buddy - a special pat for him -

XX Tinky

6 June 2006

"Another partial letter. 'Tinky' – that was her nickname. I think her parents used to call her 'Little Tinky Lou. I wonder who Burpie

& Widgie were? Must be cats. Mom loved cats. I know Buddy was her dog...'"

Silence. I closed my eyes and took a deep breath and shook my head. I had a vision of dog and cat dishes nestled together on the floor in the kitchen at grandpa and Allie's house on Cottage St, where mom grew up. I could smell Allie's cooking in the air.

"I don't know what to say: there's so much running through my head! I once asked her if she was afraid while overseas. I mean this was the woman who wouldn't leave her house, was frightened driving around New Bedford, and had heart palpitations when I drove her up to visit me! And yet she traveled through India and Africa and Israel and so many places!"

"Her answer? She said 'Oh no dear, I wasn't afraid. I was with your father.' That was it. That was her entire answer!"

I looked around the office for the Kleenex, glancing at the small clock on the top of my therapist's desk, relieved that I had time left.

"Can you pass me that Kleenex box? This one's empty. Do you charge extra for heavy snifflers?"

I blew my nose and looked around for the wastebasket. My therapist passed it over to me.

"She spoke of him like the love of her life. Yet in her letter to her parents she calls him a 'nice husband' and says she 'kind of' misses not having him around. That's so anemic sounding."

I took a breath.

"Yes; I do think she was afraid of her parents. In fact it's sad to hear her mention Buddy."

I had a vision of a picture of mom, looking healthy and happy, in a dress with a long billowing skirt, sitting on the back steps at Cottage St, petting a cocker spaniel.

"Oh why? Grandpa put him down while she was gone because he barked too much. She didn't find out until she got home."

As I sat there a heavy feeling overcame me. I felt pulled down towards the ground. Gravity had gotten stronger while I sat.

"She was the keeper of many secrets, I think."

My forehead hurt. I felt like my eyebrows were too heavy.

"I don't know who she was."

I looked around me for something familiar to hold onto. My arms and legs felt detached, my head strangely set on my shoulders. I heard my therapist reminding me to breathe. I reached inside me to communicate my feelings:

"I feel depressed…angry, sad…lost."

"I miss her."

"I loved her."

"At times I hated her."

I could feel the tears welling up against the dam of my eyeballs again, ready to spill over and down my cheeks.

"Do you have another box of Kleenex?"

I took a handful for the road, knowing that I would cry most of the way home. I paid enough for the therapy, so a few Kleenex should be included in that bill!

"Yes, it's time to go. See you Thursday."

8 June 2006 – 3 am

I live in two worlds
One world is the world
that everyone else sees
I see it too
It is through a window
As an observer
I participate, go through the motions
I eat
I laugh
I interview for a new job
I perform well at my current one
But it's the other world I'm really in
The world that no-one else sees
That only I feel
A world of loss
An aching hurt
An emptiness
The world for me has changed
The birds still sing
The sun still shines
But I am lost in it all
And sometimes can do nothing

But then I push on
For the world will change again
But it will never be the same

26 June 1949

June 26th

Dear Folks,

I thought you might be interested in this article on Kowloon where the Peninsula Hotel is. We've made two trips by ferry to Hong Kong Island, but so far the sun hasn't been out for taking pictures or looking around. The island is separated from the mainland by a channel not much more than ¼ mile wide and has 32 sq. mile area.

We just had a little excitement - two bats flew into our room - one beat it out again, but the other seems to have adopted us & is flying merrily around - I wish he'd go home!

Tonight we saw the Marx Bros. in "Casablanca", & it had some good laughs in it. This noon a Jewish family, friends of Ted

Stern, invited us to lunch. It was very nice of them to do it, but that darn highly- seasoned Jewish food gave our stomachs a wallop and it was a bit too reminiscent of Tel-Aviv! It's good to see so many Anglo Saxon faces as there are in Hong Kong, & the Chinese are very pleasant people themselves. There are a lot of native shops around the hotel district. The shopkeepers love to bargain & never expect you to pay the original price they ask. But I'm so used to our way of shopping at home that I'm a poor bargainer.

We still have our daughter with us - it does take away some of your privacy but can't be helped, as there's no other available room yet.

We're having our teak wood desk & chest shipped to you to keep for us until we've a home for them in Everett. Please uncrate them & stick them around where you choose. Since they're coming by boat, it may be six weeks before they arrive. We'd be interested in knowing the condition they arrive in, since the shop where we bought then will take care of any damage from transportation. We'd like eventually to order a teak wood dining-room set from the same factory, but are going to wait first & see how the desk & chest stand up in the change of climate. Maguire has bought some before & says it's apt to crack & give at the seams. Ours is well made with interlocking joining instead of nails, so we're hoping it will stand up better than most. We have the address of the factory, & when we're settled in Everett & know the size & shape furniture we want, we have only to send measurement & descriptions & have sets made up here. I've never liked any furniture so well & do hope it proves practical.

I'm using my new parker 51 - Herb got me a blue pen & pencil set here. Everything is cheaper than the States. You can get beautiful watches - Blackie got himself a solid gold Swiss one for $190. That would be $250-$300 at least in the States, & Herb is going to get a Universal Geneva before we leave. Then we'd better all beat it back to Tel-Aviv before we're dead broke!

Much love to all,

X Tinky X

---

8 June 2006

"She did like Parker pens! I remember that from my childhood. It feels so good to connect a memory with the woman I'm reading about here.

I looked up at my therapist. She was looking at me with a quizzical look on her face, urging me to say more.

"I think Dad liked the Marx brothers. I don't really know! That feels so frustrating!"

The sun was streaming in the window but the warmth of the outdoors hadn't penetrated the room yet. I felt hollow and cold as I looked down at the letter in my lap.

"What a mistress of understatement – that bat must have been driving her crazy! But she sat there writing a letter with it still in the room! Perhaps it was her way of escaping the present?"

I moved my fingers over the wrinkles on the airline paper parchment, feeling the years that had gone by, looking again in awe that my mother's handwriting was there – a part of her still surviving.

"I wonder what on earth she meant by 'our daughter'? Dad hadn't been over there long enough to have a child there and Peggy was back in the States. Must have been someone else's child they were looking after. Confusing."

I felt so angry that all I had left was this letter in front of me. Angry that there was so little in it. I turned it over as if more would come out from under it.

"I don't want to hear about teak furniture! I want to know what she was feeling!"

My therapist's voice murmured in a calming way that I sounded angry.

"Yes I'm angry, I almost shouted back, "I have so many swings of emotion when I read these letters. I get happy to see her handwriting. I get mad at her for not saying more. I am fascinated by what she describes and curious to find out more. I get sad that's she's gone. I cling to each page as a part of her. Sounds like a movie review, hey? They laughed, they cried, they danced in the aisles…!"

I stopped and looked around the room, feeling drained.

"I'm tired…so very tired."

I wanted to stop but as I surreptitiously glanced at the clock I saw there was time left so I pulled out another letter:

May 1949

The Sabbath May

Dear Mom & Dad,

It's definite now that we'll be leaving here May 19th or 20th. There are 250 more Adenites to be transported. Since 50 come on each flight, that means 5 more trips to Aden. Then immigration here is being halted for three months. The place is terribly over-crowded & there have been unemployment demonstrations. Maguire is due back from Shanghai tomorrow or Monday, & he & Herb will map out the route home, probably by way of Paris, Scotland, Iceland, Canada

& to New York. Blackie Bradshaw's home is in Montreal, so we're going to stop off there & let him show us around. We'll be coming on the 46.

Mrs. Maguire & I are going to visit Jerusalem the flight of next week, while Herb is off on a flight. He's quite anxious for me to see it & won't have the chance to take me himself. Then he's planning to take me along on the 2 or 3 remaining trips to Aden. The past couple of days I've been swimming in the Mediterranean here - with Mrs. Maguire & with Herb when he's here. The beach is within walking distance from the hotel, & the water is clear & warm with nice surf. We have people up to our room each night & make snacks from our canned goods supply. We both get a lot of fun from our entertaining, & Herb says it's giving the fellows a taste of home life that's quite novel to them. It's lovely & cool here morning &

night, getting quite warm during the day. The rainy season ended just before I got here & now each day is sunny - the sky & water a bright blue. We'll be leaving before the really hot weather settles in - & I guess it gets plenty hot!

We have breakfast sent up to the room each morning & are fortunate that we can get eggs at the hotel. Then I do my ironing & what little housekeeping there's need of, & then to the beach.

I sure do look forward to that daily swim & am getting quite a tan. Herb hasn't been in yet but he sits on the beach & watches.

I don't know how long we'll have in the East when we return - maybe a day, maybe a week. I don't know how long we'll be stopping over in Paris or Scotland to break the trip, but we should be back in the States around May 25-28. We'll cable you definitely when we will be arriving.

I'm glad I came over mainly because I've had an initiation into the flight game that I'd probably never have obtained otherwise or any place else. It was a bit rough at first, but worth it! The fellows say they're glad I came because Herb was one unhappy fellow without me. He's getting a lot of rest & looks a hundred percent better. We're both well & happy, & these few weeks together here have been an experience we'll never forget. A bit different from the usual honeymoon - but interesting & fun! Love to all, Tinky X

---

8 June 2006

"How do I feel? I have so many questions left unanswered: I wonder if she did get to Montreal? It would have been great to talk about that when I was working in Montreal!"

I hurried on to avoid feeling the loss.

"Her comment about the boys saying that Dad was miserable there without her is so cute. I do believe that they were very much in love. She never remarried. Said she never found anyone who could take Dad's place."

My mind wandered to being in the living room at 85 Armour St. with mom. Through my brain flitted a vague memory of her speaking about Dad. I must have been around 2 or 3. I rushed on to avoid being caught by the memory.

"All the talk about Everett in her previous letters and now saying they may only be one day on the East Coast. I was assuming Everett was in MA and Dad was going to be based at Logan but perhaps there's another Everett. I know they ended up living in Abington MA around the time that I was born."

My mind drifted to visiting Dad and my step-mom, Kit, in Arlington and riding a bike I got for Xmas in their apartment complex cellar. I continued talking faster to race back to the present.

"There must have been a lot of hopes being raised towards going home and then dashed again as they got extended for mom. I wonder if she ended up hating it there?"

The past was threatening to overwhelm me with a dank blackness of hurt and lost hope. I reached into my backpack and almost threw the next show and tell pieces at my therapist. I knew she knew what game I was playing but was glad she wasn't calling me on it today. The clock seemed to have stopped as I waded against the pull of my past worlds. There was so much time to fill.

"I found these two telegrams that she sent home. It's really neat to see a real telegram. I've never seen one before! It also shows how near they got towards going home when the plans were changed. They were really being jerked around. I guess that was part of the business though and perhaps what mom couldn't take about being married to an airline pilot."

2 August 1949

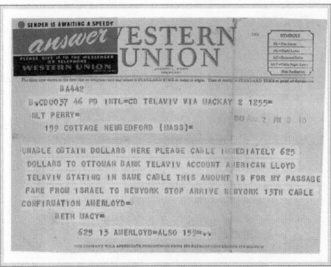

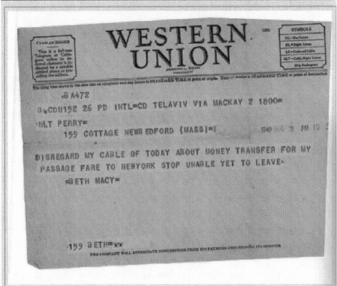

8 June 2006

I started talking very quickly, the sound of my voice irritating to my ears. This wasn't what I wanted to be talking about. I wanted to check in with me but I couldn't stop the prattle!

"Dad hated to swim. His dad taught him to swim by throwing him in. He could swim but he rarely did it. Mom loved to swim. She did the breaststroke and dog paddle. And boy could she tan! She always was a bit dismayed by her two children who burned! We curbed her sun exposure for a while!"

My mind raced on, the intellect completely in control of the emotions.

"Mom talks about the overcrowding and unemployment demonstrations. Tom Segev in his book[7] also talks about these issues, saying that 'total unemployment in Israel including the new immigrants, stood at 14 percent.' He also writes about a local council in Raanana who wrote: 'The town councils are filled each day with hundreds of people shouting, "Bread and Work!" '

I avoided looking at my therapist as the words spilled out of my mouth.

"And he writes about debates going on within Israel about slowing the immigration and/or changing the selection for those to be allowed in. My step-mom recalls that in the US there were debates going on as to whether they should give money to help build Israel or not. It seems clear that the rate of immigration was

---

7   *1949: The First Israelis*, by Tom Segev

faster than the ability to absorb the new immigrants. I do wish I had more information about the timelines and what went on."

My stomach had a familiar ache in it. I heard my therapist reminding me to breathe. I prattled on:

"Dad never spoke of this either, but I also didn't know to ask him. He was one of those guys who when he returned home from a trip where the weather was horrid or there was mechanical difficulties or the like, he'd just say, 'I took the plane from point A to point B successfully and that's what it's all about.'"

I smiled, remembering Dad sitting at the kitchen table in his Kingston home, drawling in his New England accent, smoking a Marlboro.

"I remember the last check-up he had down at Dallas when he was close to retiring. He went down there to do the 3-day evaluation in the simulator. He came home in two days and the family was petrified to ask what happened. We didn't want to hear that he had failed. So finally I said, 'Hey Dad, how come you're back early?' He smiled and dryly said 'They're going to have to change the test.' I looked at him quizzically and he smiled again, more broadly, and said 'Finished it in two days.' That was my dad – blew away the 3-day simulation test they give the pilots in 2 days! He was an excellent pilot!"

The smile took over my whole face as I puffed up with pride for having had him as a dad. The tears weren't far behind. I talked on.

"He had wanted to start his own charter company after retirement but they told him when he went for his lump sum retirement that he couldn't get it because he had high blood pressure and then he was grounded. I think that killed him more than anything else. He loved flying."

Finally my therapist pointed out the time. I looked up. She was smiling. I knew in that look that I hadn't fooled her. But I also knew that it was ok to be where I was today - that the emotions would work their way out in these sessions. The room looked clearer than it usually did. The sun was shining in the window.

"We've run over? Sorry... OK, see you next week."

Undated – sometime in 1949

Sunday A.M.

Dear Folks,

Rain again today, but I guess we're lucky to have had it since we came, for they say the heat is terrific when it's not raining. Last night Maguire, Herb & I took the ferry over to Hong Kong Island. We're staying in Kowloon on the mainland. We had dinner at the Parisian

Grill, where there' supposed to be the best food in town, & they give you a T-bone steak the size of a platter, but the steak is better here at the hotel, & I'm going to have steak until it's coming out my ears, since we can't get any in Tel-Aviv. Green salads & vegetables are good, too, & I wish we had longer here - for the improved diet is doing us worlds of good. We took a small launch for the ride back to the mainland. It was a lovely ride, with the freighters lighted up in the harbor & the lights from shore.

Maguire is going back with us to Tel-Aviv. He's written an extension complaint to Marshall in New York - owner & financial backer of Alaska Airlines - about the lack of funds sent to run the operations here, lack of business office

(Mrs. Maguire found it as distressing as I have to have your hotel room used as an office), lack of bookkeeper & secretary. Herb had to run several charter cash-payment trips to Asmara to get sufficient funds to pay hotel & taxi bills. I mentioned the fact several times in Tel-Aviv that I thought the home office was planting men overseas & pretty much forgetting about them, & I'm rather glad to have Maguire bring the same thing to Herb's attention. If sufficient provisions aren't made for the running of these overseas operations, Maguire has written Marshall that he can accept his resignation. I think Maguire, & Herb also, is too valuable a man for them to lose & that his letter will bring results. I've been acting as bookkeeper & secretary for the Tel-Aviv end; Mrs. Maguire did the same things for the Hong Kong deal. I didn't mind doing it because I had the time. But the main complaint is the lack of finances from New York to pay bills & local crew & the lack of definite instructions. C.A.B. has closed down on Alaska here because the scheduled airlines complained that Alaska was taking business away from them. We're starting on a new operation in Tel-Aviv, which, as I gather, involves flying into Saudi-Arabia. Since Alaska has been flying the Jewish refugees, our C46 wouldn't be too welcome there, so it has supposedly been leased from Alaska by a new company, headed by Maguire as President. If we're to be there for 6 months or so, Bob is sending for his wife & children, & we'll all see about getting decent living quarters & flying in meat, canned milk, Nescafe', fruit, vegetables, etc., for our own use. This is all provided that Alaska pays Bob & Herb sufficiently high salaries to warrant their staying in a place where living costs are as high as they are in Tel-Aviv. It's about 10 cents to have a shirt laundered here & it's ready for you in a few hours. It's $.75 to $1.00 to have a shirt laundered in Tel-Aviv, & you're lucky if you get it in a few days. A lunch in Hong Kong, with fruit cocktail, steak, vegetables, salad, & milk will cost about 75 cents. A lunch in Tel-Aviv, with potato soup, a bit of fried fish or veal, potatoes, and cabbage will cost you about $2.00. Some diff!!

We were going to take advantage of being in a non-Jewish community & go to church this morning. But when I called the desk at 10 A.M. to find out about Protestant churches, the only one she knew of was an Episcopalian nearby where the service began at 10 A.M. So Herb has gone to the airport to see how they're coming along on the plane, & I guess our little old C46 is getting a thorough beauty treatment. They're covering the skeleton inside

with plush lining; taking out the bucket seats
& putting in two rows of arm seats; and - above
all - taking out the tiny, wobbly can we had
in the back for a "biffy" & mirror; and also
they're going to fix the door to the toilet so it
will close from the inside! It just won't seem
like home any more!

Herb and I have an adopted daughter! When
the 54 Maguire came on got in the other day,
there was no room at the hotel for one of the
stewardesses. Since we couldn't stick her in with
Maguire or the spare bed in Ford, Blackie &
Ted's room, we offered to take her in with us.
(We've a large room & four beds.) She's very nice
& a quiet girl -much more wholesome than the
general run of bags that go in for stewardess-
ing. So we have her with us to guard her virtue,
but it

13 June 2006

It was raining outside, a damp drizzling unsatisfying rain, whose only purpose was to dampen my mood. I felt angry as I looked down at the letter in my lap.

"That's it. That's where it ends! Amazing!"

I sat stiffly on the couch in silence, feeling the anger bubble beneath the surface, waiting to retrieve the next batch of words from my mind. It was if I had a whirlpool of thoughts swirling around and a net out to catch bits of them as they whirled by, twisting and turning, attempting to avoid capture.

"What's amazing? That she could run the bookkeeping and secretarial part of an operation! That she was going to eat steak until it came out of her ears! I didn't even know my mother knew what steak was! She was an anorexic toothpick!"

I sat again in silence. Visions of my mom cooking in that tiny one-person kitchen at Armour St, with me sitting on top of the refrigerator so I could be with her, floated by in my thoughts. Smells wafted through my brain as I searched for what she cooked and ate.

"I remember though growing up that she loved liver and onions. She'd cook liver and onions and bacon. She used to cook at one time. She made her own bread and mayonnaise – even wonderful perfect popovers! I think the electric bill scared her in her later years and she stopped cooking."

Silence again. I remembered sitting in the dining room making mayonnaise with mom as the tough taskmaster ensuring the oil went in drop by drop. And I swore I could smell the bread dough rising by the hot water pipe in the towel cabinet.

"There's such a break between who she was and who she became!"

I sat on the couch with my head down and fists clenched. My therapist's question gently intruded into my thoughts.

"Angry? Yes I'm angry – this woman sounds almost normal! Of course she's as judgmental and prejudiced as always!"

I rocked back and forth a bit as I struggled with being fair to who mom was.

"But I can relate to her at times here! In a way, I'll always have part of mom through her letters. I'm typing them up. She had started to do it but only typed up a couple. So I figure she'd like for me to type them up for her."

Silence.

"Can I have a Kleenex?"

I stared at the box, unwilling to let the tears flow again, feeling them welled up behind my eyeballs, resisting the flood.

"I just feel so sad…it helps to work on researching her past though…"

I quickly switched topics, and saw my therapist make a note on her notepad.

"I found more information on the web about the Yemenites.[8] In this article Ya'akov Meron claims that the Arab rulers coordinated the expulsion of Jews from Arab territory. He claims that the Iraq government planned the expulsion of the Jews in 1949 and goes on to talk about other areas that also did, including Yemen."

"Here's the article:"

---

8   http://www.meforum.org/article/263

Similar patterns of Jewish exodus existed in other Arabic-speaking countries, including Yemen, Libya, Syria, Egypt, Algeria and Jordan.

Yemen. Yemeni persecution of Jews prompted a trickle of Jewish emigration to Palestine from the third quarter of the nineteenth century on. Heykal Pasha's speech merely added momentum to the longstanding Yemeni policy of discrimination against and degradation of Jews, based on a particularly pedantic interpretation of the Islamic law. A bribe from the American Joint Distribution Committee to Yemen's ruler, Imam Ahmad ibn Yahya, led to his agreeing to the mass exodus of Jews to Israel in 1949-50 by airplane via Aden, an operation known as "On Eagle's Wings" (or, in journalistic lore, "Magic Carpet"). The Jews of Yemen, relying on their own means, suffering losses of life and deprivations, traversed the desert to Aden by foot and on donkeys. There, the Jewish Agency lodged them in camps and eventually boarded them onto planes that took them to Israel. In this way, some 50,000 Yemeni Jews reached Israel during the two-year period.

We lack information about the Yemeni government's decision-making process. But this case provides the clearest example of Jews' being persecuted and expelled for reasons having to do with Islamic law.

"He goes on to say that there is a silence about this expulsion of Jews:"

On the Israeli side, the establishment did little to break the silence about the dire circumstances of the Jewish exodus from Arab countries. 40[9]

---

9   40 Mordekhaï Ben-Porat is one exception,: at the end of 1975, he established the World Organization of Jews from Arab Countries. He also spoke up on this topic in the Israeli parliament (see, for example, Divrei ha-Knesset, vol. 72, Jan. 1, 1975, p. 1112).

Quite the contrary, the romantic "magic carpet" image for the migration from Yemen and the "Ezra and Nehemiah Operation" name attached to the Iraqi migration stress the positive, glossing over the unhappy circumstances of the Arab expulsions. Jean-Pierre Péroncel-Hugoz, a French orientalist and journalist at Le Monde, notes with surprise "that Israel only very rarely emphasizes the fact that a part of its population left property and space it legitimately owned in the Arab countries of its origin."41[10]

"So he goes on to claim that the Arabs forced the Jews out of their homes and in resettling the Jews forced the Arabs out of their homes."

What happened, therefore, is merely a kind of 'population and property transfer,' the consequences of which both sides have to bear. Thus Israel gathers in the Jews from Arab countries and the Arab countries are obliged in turn to settle the Palestinians within their own borders and work towards a solution of the problem".

---

10   41 Jean-Pierre Péroncel-Hugoz, Une Croix sur le Liban (Paris: Lieu Commun, 1984), p. 114. The issue of Jewish refugees from Arab countries is likely to grow in importance as many of their number reach the forefront of public life in Israel. In the imd-1980s, for example, the chief of staff of the Israel army, the parliamentary speaker, the minister of justice, the minister of energy, and the minister of health all were of Iraqi origin. The secretary-general of the Histadrut (the labor federation) was born in Yemen. The deputy prime minister and the minister of the interior were born in Morocco. The countries of the Arab League have by now an impressive representation in the government of Israel.

"Fascinating? Isn't it?"

I looked up and saw my therapist sitting and waiting for me to acknowledge what I had done.

"I know I changed the subject. It gets too painful at times to look at my feelings."

"Our time's up already?"

"Sigh..."

"OK, I'll see you Thursday".

I drove home with my fingers clenched on the steering wheel, angry at myself that I had paid so much money for a session where I avoided my feelings. I knew I was avoiding writing things down outside of the sessions too. I had done no writing last week. I pounded a fist on the steering wheel and started crying. I drove over the bridge home with my surroundings a blur of tears, anger and sadness rolled into one.

10 June 2007

The phone ring burst through the silence. I jumped up, knocking the book off my lap, and as I did so I reminded myself there was no longer any reason to fear that ring. I stood, my feet leaden and unwilling to move further, paralyzed by tears in the middle of the living room, the phone ringing shrilly. There was no longer a reason to answer it.

I picked up the receiver too late and started listening to the messages. An old one from mom was on the machine. The shock of hearing her voice rippled through me. "Call me dear." Oh mom, I so wish I could.

10 June 1949

June 10th

Saturday

*YARDEN HOTEL/130, BEN-YEHUDA St.,
TEL-AVIV / PHONE 3732*

Dear Folks,

I've just received a cable that Wooten is arriving Tuesday & we're to remain in Tel-Aviv - for how long, I don't know. What a life! We were hoping to get to Hong Kong before another contract was dropped in our laps, but it looks like we're too late.

At least we'll have to take the plane to Amsterdam for maintenance before any more work can be done here.

Now I'm off to get some sun & surf - bathing on the beach.

XX Tinky XX

---

15 June 2006

"Well that's short and sweet..."

I paused and looked at my therapist, waiting for her to lead.

"Am I disappointed? Yes I feel disappointed – I want more!"

I set the letter down and looked up again. The room around my therapist's head was blurred and distant, it was as if space had shrunk to just the two of us. I heard her ask me how I was feeling.

"So how am I feeling? Angry that there isn't more. Empty, wanting to fill the void. I eat and don't feel full. I fall asleep but I don't feel rested. I just feel tired and sad and empty and angry!"

I sat still for a moment, feeling empty, drained, and then reached for another letter from my backpack. These letters were all that I had left of my mother. I wanted more from them than they could give me, but it was a connection. I didn't want to let go of her world. She was alive in that past. Both mom and Dad were. I wanted to join them there.

1 June 1949

June 1ˢᵗ on the C46 - 3 ½ hrs. out from Lydda

Dear Folks,

This has been a long day - starting at 4:30 this morning when the houseboy brought us tea at the Crescent Hotel in Aden to wake us up. We left the airport in Aden about 6:15 for Djibouti. Djibouti is as hot as Aden & quite a dump. We had breakfast at the leading hotel there, but it looked like the cockroaches were ready to walk out & shake hands with you.

Anyway, we had steak & (tough & unappetizing!) eggs for breakfast, also salad & some very good dry red wine, for which Djibouti is apparently famous. I took some pictures, too, so you'll get a chance to see what it was like. One of those places that it's interesting to see once - but once is enough.

Last night in Aden we went swimming after supper & that is a treat. The water's very warm, but you do feel a bit cooler afterwards. We'll reach Lydda Airport around 6 tonight.

Later: - at Tel-Aviv.

Am enclosing some pictures that had just come back & were waiting here at the hotel.

XX Tinky X

15 June 2006

I looked at my therapist and then again at the letter and shook my head: "I didn't find any pictures in the envelope."

I held up the letter in front of me and shook it, and then spoke to the letter: "You were a real person in these letters mom! It was before you started hiding under your wig and behind layers of pancake makeup."

A vision of mom sitting in her wheelchair, small and frail, in the nursing home edged its way into my head. I shook my head trying to erase that image and think of her in earlier days.

"Funny, as I was reading this one I could almost smell your scent – the combination of perfume, hand-lotion and make-up."

I could see her bureau at Armour Street in my mind, cluttered with jars and bottles, a dim reflection of her in the mirror, and those smells mingling, nail-polish, foundation, lipstick, perfume, overwhelming my senses. I tried to relocate that dim image and imagine her sitting in a plane. She was always so afraid when I flew anywhere.

"Were you bored on those flights? Frightened? I can't get any sense of it…"

I put the letter down and looked at my therapist and then around the small room, seeing the clock hands reach the hour. I shook my head again. Everything looked foreign and out of place.

"Nothing makes sense…"

I heard my therapist point out the time and stood up to leave.

"OK – Until Tuesday…"

20 June 2006

I sat silently while my therapist read what I had handed her. I knew the opening words by heart:

Yesterday my sister lost her best friend. I lost the most complex relationship I will ever have. I've spent 30 years and thousands of dollars in therapy trying to understand myself, my mother's world, and my place in relationship to it...

I nervously watched my therapist's face, looking for clues to what she'd ask me, hearing the scratch of her pen as she made notes on her pad of paper. I played with the stuffed bear that had been perched on the top of the couch, making it do cartwheels on my lap. She handed the typewritten pages back to me and asked me when I wrote it.

"I wrote that the night after she died. I couldn't sleep. I had to let it out. It just flowed – just like that! I got up in the middle of the night and typed it all in. Then I read it at her funeral. Someone had to say something real about her. The minister was on his last legs and couldn't even remember mom's name! Deb was too distraught to do anything."

I hugged the bear to my chest, a defense against being probed too closely.

"I sound angry again? Hum, I guess I am. I'm angry at her for dying. I'm angry at not having a real family – at all the past junk between us – at having to pay $7K for the funeral."

I paused as my mind raced through the events of that day again, seeing the flowers sent by my co-workers and friends, my sister holding court with her friends, feeling outcast until my friends showed up from traveling far to get there, feeling lost and alone.

"Deb thanked me for the funeral…"

I felt anger well up, feeling used, having done what was expected of me, the responsible one.

"It wasn't for her. I did it for mom."

I softened as I thought of my mother living her last years in that little one bedroom hovel I had bought her with mice in the cupboards and termites in the foundation, while I lived in my three bedroom house on the North Shore.

"It was the least I could do."

I heard my therapist tell me that not many children buy houses for their parents.

"Perhaps I did too much, but I just feel like I've always done too little."

"Yes, I'll do some writing this week."

"See you Thursday."

24 May 1949

May 24th

Dear Folks,

Enclosed is a shot taken in the park here in Tel-Aviv. They turned out pretty well.

I wasn't being formal when I signed my full name to your telegram - they won't send them with just a first name.

Much love to all - keep writing -

Tinky XX

May 24th

Yesterday two wires arrived from Maguire, instructing us to clean up this area & go on to Hong Kong. There are eight more trips scheduled here from Aden, Asmara & Djibouiti. The alternate crew has been taking the last three in a row to let Herb run the business end here.

Guess they need the C46 for flying refugees from Shanghai to Hong Kong. We'll be through here in about two weeks. I can't say I'll be sorry to leave Tel-Aviv. I sent you a cable yesterday that we'd be leaving for Hong Kong.

Loads & loads of love to all,

Tinky XX

22 June 2006

I took the envelope back from my therapist, and showed her another envelope.

"This envelope had actually been opened by the censors and resealed with a red tape. None of the others had been taped that way. It looks like she took out all the pictures when she reread them or else her folks had removed them. All the pictures I found were lying around in different drawers when I cleaned out the house."

9 June 1949

June 9th

YARDEN HOTEL/130, BEN-YEHUDA St., TEL-AVIV / PHONE 3732

Dear Mum & Dad,

Our leaving for Hong Kong keeps being postponed, as additional trips to Aden & Asmara come up. There's one more Aden flight scheduled & the possibility of one more to Asmara.

However, Herb says we should be leaving here in five days maximum. Tomorrow we're going to Haifa to see about the visas we'll need for Pakistan, India and Hong Kong.

Went to the beach this noon, but the waves are high now, so you can't do much swimming.

Not much news, but just a line to let you know we are well and still in Tel-Aviv.

Lots of love to all,

Tinky X

22 June 2006

"All these places I need to look up on the map! I realize how little I really know about that area of the world. I didn't think of the Mediterranean as having waves but it's a large sea so I guess it would! I looked up on the web to get more information. I found out that the Mediterranean doesn't have tides and is saltier than the Atlantic Ocean. It also is nice and warm compared to the

Atlantic here in New England![11] No wonder mom enjoyed swimming in it!"

I pulled myself out of their world and back to my reality. I felt drained again.

"I want to know so much but have so little energy to find it out. And mom and Dad can no longer tell me. It seems so futile..."

My therapist commented that I looked tired. I paused and looked down at my hands to connect myself to my body and check in.

"Yes I'm very tired. I'm not sleeping well yet."

I felt so old inside - flat, hollow, void of life and joy.

"It seems like it was only yesterday that she died. But everyone seems to act as if I should be over it all."

Memories floated through my head of cleaning out mom's house, driving furniture in a U-Haul over to my sister Deb's house, following the hearse to the grave, of sitting in my car in the driveway at home and crying so hard I could hardly breathe...

"I know, a month isn't a long time at all..."

I paused again and felt nothing, saw nothing, had nothing to offer.

"I don't know what else to say."

I could feel the tears well up again, silently starting to stream down my cheeks.

"Can I have a Kleenex, please?"

---

11   http://www.1911encyclopedia.org/Mediterranean_Sea

I glanced at the clock and saw we were almost out of time so reached for what else I could say before I left. The sentences peppered my departure as I stood up to leave.

"I'll do some writing…it does help. There's so much going through my head that I can hardly keep up with it. And then sometimes I don't want to feel at all because it hurts so much."

"And I'm so sick of crying…"

"How do I feel right now?"

"Angry…strange that should pop up when I'm crying…but I'm sick of all this. I've had close to 18 months of crying. It's time for something good to happen."

"Ah shit…. I miss her so…"

"Yes I'll see you next week. Thanks."

23 June 2006 – 3am

I miss being able to ask my mother for advice.

I remember visiting her in the nursing home and looking at that leathered old face with the almost blind watery eyes and wondering where my mother had gone. Where she had slipped to over the years? Where was that woman I could relate to – the one who bought cars, took out mortgages, went to work? The one I could ask for advice – what to do with a bad cut, or a stomachache, or a lousy job.

And I read her diary from high school and the letters she wrote home from overseas and I see first a spoiled self-indulgent young woman who is very tied to New Bedford and home and then a much more self reliant woman who wandered half way around the world with my dad.

And then I remember the mother who was both loving and caring and tough and out of control. Who dragged her children out of school so she'd have company on sales trips to Boston. As a child of around 10 years old, I'd navigate for her and light her cigarettes so she could keep two hands on the wheel, tightly clenching it, white knuckled driving through the unfamiliar Boston traffic.

I think she lost her support system over the years and sank more and more into avoiding discomfort. It became very hard for me to relate to the woman of latter years, to the woman who preached to me when I was young:

> Tender Hearted Touch a Nettle
> And it will sting you for your pains
> But grasp it like a Man of Mettle
> And it soft as silk remains

I so wish I could pick up the phone and call her wherever she now is...

---

27 June 2006

"Look I found this on the web:"
I handed the printout to my therapist.

Israel's History:1949[12]

1949:by Michal Kabatznik, 2002-2003 Hanegev Israel Affairs VP

In the year 1949 Israel was just starting out as a state. Here are some of the events taking place there in 1949.

*   * In January a cease-fire agreement was signed with Egypt, Syria, and Lebanon.*

*   * Israel's first democratic elections were held on January 25th. Chaim Weizmann was elected president, while David Ben Gurion formed a government as Israel's first Prime Minister.*

*   * In April Jordan signed a cease-fire as well as taking Jerusalem. Jerusalem would remain in Jordanian hands until the Six Day War in 1967.*

*   * Operation "Magic Carpet" begins bringing Yemenite and Moroccan Jews to Israel.*

*   * On May 13th Israel was admitted to the United Nations. 37 nations voted in favor, 12 opposed, and 9 abstained.*

*   * On September 18th, Theodore Herzl's remains were brought to Israel and reburied at Har Herzl military cemetery in Jerusalem.*

*   * On November 7th, Jerusalem was declared as Israel's official capital.*

"That guy was Israel's first Prime Minister! I wonder if mom met him?"

"What am I getting out of these letters? I do feel like I've been given a gift to help me heal; to be able to see through her eyes; to understand her more. There are tidbits in these letters that remind

---

12 http://www.usy.org/yourusy/israel/timeline/1949.asp

me of the mother whom I knew at times growing up. And she now has a past. She just seems like a fuller person, and in some way alive again. Or at least part of her is living on here in these letters."

"And I found Bob Maguire's obituary too:"

By Dennis McLellan, Los Angeles Times | June 18, 2005[13]

LOS ANGELES – Robert F. Maguire Jr., the commercial pilot from Oregon who was called the "Irish Moses" for helping fly tens of thousands of Jewish refugees through hostile territory from Yemen to Israel in 1949, has died. He was 94.

Mr. Maguire died of natural causes June 10 at his home in the Northridge section of Los Angeles, his family said.

The World War II veteran was working for Alaska Airlines in late 1948, when the company was contracted by the American Joint Distribution Committee to fly Jewish refugees from Yemen, where they had been oppressed for centuries, to the newly established state of Israel.

As the chief pilot of Operation Magic Carpet, Mr. Maguire helped transport more than 40,000 refugees on nearly 400 flights, a successful airlift that prompted David Ben-Gurion, prime minister of Israel, to call Mr. Maguire the "Irish Moses."

The operation was a secret one – it was feared that the planes would be shot down by Arab forces, who were at war with Israel – but while they were often shot at, none of the planes crashed, and no lives were lost.

The flights began at Asmara in Eritrea and flew to Aden, where the pilots picked up passengers and delivered them to Tel Aviv, 1,500 miles north.

---

13 http://www.fresh.co.il/vBulletin/showthread.php?t=118498

The pilots, who flew close to the ground and moved in and out of passes and valleys to avoid detection, then flew to Cyprus for the night.

The round trip lasted 15 to 20 hours, with as many as 28 pilots flying at any one time.

After several months, Alaska Airlines withdrew from the operation. Mr. Maguire, who had a wife and three children in Tel Aviv at the time, said last year that the company had been logging too many flight hours and could have been penalized by the Federal Aviation Administration.

But that wasn't the end of the airlift operation: Mr. Maguire kept it going by buying or leasing planes and setting up Near East Air Transport.

He said he was motivated more by the adventure than the money.

But there was more to his commitment to the airlift than that for Mr. Maguire, whose father was a judge in the Nuremberg war-crimes trials after World War II.

Mr. Maguire never forgot the Yemenites' singing and blessing as they flew into Israel, nor the grateful expressions on their faces.

"It was so touching you almost don't want to remember," he recalled.

27 June 2006

I took the printout back from my therapist.

"The Maguire obituary gives a lot of information! Dad & Mom did that too!"

My mind raced ahead, words jumbled with feelings, all going too fast to capture. I shook my head and said: "Amazing…"

I heard my therapist ask how I was feeling and reminding me to breathe.

"I feel angry that they weren't written up somewhere; that their story wasn't told. Just because Dad wasn't a suck-up to the airlines I bet. There's a deeper story underneath all this."

I sat quietly for a moment, feeling my insides scramble to catch up with the emotions running through. Sadness won.

"Sigh...I'll probably never know it all. I wish I had them back to ask."

I thought of all those nights, sitting in a cloud of cigarette smoke, talking at the kitchen table with Dad when I was in college, of questions left unasked, of questions that I didn't know enough to ask; of the years growing up with mom with no questions asked; of lost opportunities.

"Thanks for the Kleenex."

I sat quietly and shut the doors in my brain to exploring further. I was sick of looking for what couldn't be found, of crying, of feeling lost, of feeling angry.

"Yes I feel very sad. Angry, sad, confused...frustrated...lost... and angry again."

I could feel the thoughts and feelings knocking on those shut doors, turning my stomach into a knot, making my head hurt, constricting my chest.

"There's just so much going through my head right now. I can't grasp onto any of it."

I clenched and unclenched my hands, feeling like I wanted to run far away.

"Time's up? OK."

16 June 1949

Albergo - C.I.A.A.O. - Hotel

ASMARA

(ERITRIA)   *June 16*

Dir. COMM. L. GIANFILIPPI

- - - - - - - - - - - -

Telefon i: 21 - 94 - 32 - 31

Telegra : CIAAO - Asmara

Dear Folks,

This is just a scribbled note, because they're waiting for me to get to the airport. We got into Asmara last night. We were headed for Aden but ran short on fuel - the mechanic in Tel-Aviv's fault. So now we're off for Aden. We're on our way to Hong Kong, & should be in Bombay by tomorrow night. Will write more aboard the plane.

Much love,

Tinky X

---

29 June 2006

I walked into my therapist's office, armed with my offerings, ready to keep the emotions at bay. I sat down quickly, avoiding eye contact and started reading her the first letter.

"How matter of fact. We ran short on fuel. In a two-engine plane, filled with Jewish refuges being ferried over Arab territory, that was no laughing matter! I was thinking, 'how blasé of her', until I found this other letter:"

I handed the second letter over, knowing that it would be scanned and passed back. That my therapist wanted to know what was under the letters for me, how I was reacting to them. Today I just felt scared, scared that the letters would run out, scared that I would feel this way forever, scared that I had failed to be a good daughter, scared that the wounds of my childhood and the rift between me and my mother would never heal, and scared of looking deeper inside to find the answers.

---

17 June 1949

Thursday

1:45 P.M.

aboard C46 enroute Aden

Dear Folks,

Well, here we are on our way to Hong Kong at last. We left Lydda around noon yesterday, headed for Aden. Bert the mechanic hadn't filled the tanks & no one had thought to check. When the main tanks went dry, we had just enough reserve to make a quick switch to

Asmara. I sort of held my breath till we pulled in there! Got in there about 7 at night.

How do you like my stationary? It's from my account books! This morning before leaving Asmara, the fellows got caught up on their shots for India & China. Herb & I were both up-to-date, but Tommy Reis (our mechanic) had the works, including Typhoid. So I expect he'll be laid up a bit tomorrow! We had a wild day before leaving Tel Aviv. Two 54's came through from Hong Kong with Wooten on one.

We shipped one of the 4's back to Hong Kong in the afternoon, & the other, plus Wooten, left for the States at midnight. Before they left we all had dinner at the airport, & I got a good chance to meet Wooten since I sat next to him & he kept giving me parts of his dinner because he was too tired to eat. Herb's seniority rank with the company has gone up several numbers, & Wooten was well pleased with the job he's done here. He told us to take the plane to Hong Kong for maintenance & then return to Tel-Aviv for probably 6 months further work, carrying passengers & meat. I know it's a long time to be away from the States, but by so doing, Herb is furthering his job no end. When we do return, there'll be no more extended overseas flights for him, we can make a home for ourselves in Everett, & there'll be some money in the bank. Wooten's secretary is going to open a joint account for us in Everett & start putting Herb's pay there.

Our next stop after Aden will be a little island off the coast of southeastern Arabia – Massawa;

I think it's called - then Bombay, Calcutta, Bangkok, Hong Kong.

I imagine the Axlerods called you when they got into Westover. They're a very charming couple from Johannesburg, So. Africa, whom I met through Mrs. Maguire in Tel-Aviv. They're on vacation touring the States. By the way, Mrs. Maguire went back to Everett about two weeks ago. It's not an easy life for a woman over here, particularly when you're hotel room is also Alaska Airline's office. I know the lack of privacy bothered her a good deal, as it does me. But I'm going to try & stick it out. We've broken up our house-keeping at the Yarden & are taking everything along with us, just in case we find different orders waiting at Hong Kong - knowing how Alaska Airlines changes it's plans for us! I was up all night packing, *after we've seen Wooten off we didn't get back to the hotel till 2 A.M.*

There are 6 of us making this trip to Hong Kong: - Blackie, Ford, & Herb - pilots; Ted the radio operator; Reis the mechanic - we got him from Trans Carrib.; & me - the stewardess & probably nurse when the boys' shots start to take effect.

More later & lots of love,

X Tinky X

---

29 June 2006

I took the letter back from my therapist, and commented, "That's a bit more colorful!" I wanted so for mom to paint her life for me, to give me a treasure by letting me fully walk in that world with her. I felt cheated by each letter that was superficial and didn't share fully that piece of the past and moment of history that mom and Dad were living in and creating. Lost in my own world and in mom's, I continued with my show and tell.

"I was wondering who Wooten was – he sounded influential in some way. So I did more web crawling and found information about him on Alaska's web site:"

Close to the Heart[14]

Rabbi Emeritus Herbert Morris frequently remembers Alaska's contribution to Operation Magic Carpet. He carries around a dog-eared newspaper clipping in his vest pocket. It's an obituary. And he's carried it for many years.

The obituary describes a man who "all of a sudden was involved in something greater than himself. What he did as a human being is the essence of religion and I was honoring that man's memory."

Rabbi Morris still talks reverently about the role that James Wooten (pictured at right), President of Alaska Airlines 50 years ago, played in Operation Magic Carpet – an airlift that brought thousands of Yemenite Jews to Israel to escape persecution.

"My business is knowing about the miracles that happen every day," Morris said recently from his home in San Francisco. "One of those miracles was Alaska Airlines delivering the Yemenite Jews to the land of their ancestors. That was a man doing God's holy work on this earth."

Wooten was the driver behind Alaska's participation in the airlift, and he played a key role in the logistics of the nearly year-long operation that made the mission successful despite many challenges.

"It was marvelous that a man, a group of men, stretched forth their wings and delivered the Yemenite Jews to their homeland," Morris said. "I read his obituary many years ago and realized what he had done and I've shared his contribution with many groups of people over the years. I've

---

14 http://www.alaskaair.com/www2/company/
    History/WootenMagicCarpet.asp

read that obituary to them as an example of what can be done if we put our hearts and hands to a task.

"James Wooten's memory will live on and I'll continue to fly Alaska Airlines every chance I get."

James Wooten

"I also found this snippet on the web:"

In the spring of 1950, the Mossad called in its most reliable partner for airlifting Jews–Alaska Airlines, whose president, James Wooten, had just months earlier been instrumental in rescuing the Jews of Yemen.[15]

"Seems like he was quite the influential guy. No wonder mom had that 'tone' in her letters when she wrote about him."

I hurried on to avoid any comments or questions: "Looking for information is like a treasure hunt. Bit by bit I fill in the pieces."

I looked down at my lap, avoiding my therapist's eyes and continued talking quickly.

---

15 http://www.bankingonbaghdad.com/archive/
ReformJudaism2004V33N2/black.shtml

"I was cleaning out my file cabinets and I just happened to find a package that mom had given me in February 2005 when she was 'cleaning house', thinking she was dying. In it I found a wedding invitation!"

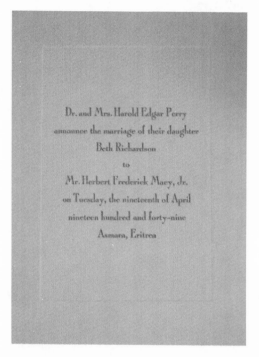

Dr. and Mrs. Harold Edgar Perry
announce the marriage of their daughter
Beth Richardson
to
Mr. Herbert Frederick Macy, Jr.
on Tuesday, the nineteenth of April
nineteen hundred and forty-nine
Asmara, Eritrea

"There it is! They must have sent one over to mom & Dad since she mentions that the invite will have everyone looking up Eritrea on their maps!"

"I found it on the globe at the Christian Science Center in Boston. That was a neat feeling. I felt like I had a secret part of that globe that no-one else recognized."

I paused from prattling on. My therapist was looking at me with that quizzical look on her face. I sent her a beseeching look asking silently to let me go on. I sighed, felt the sadness well up inside, and then spoke:

"This is all I have. This is the tie of me to her, to my past, to the puzzle that I live with of who was she, and, in a sense, who am I. I feel driven to find out everything I can."

I passed her another letter, a small piece of a precious whole. A puzzle that hopefully had all the pieces that I needed to complete it.

---

24 April 1949

Crescent Hotel

Aden

(Please excuse the mess - but the paper kept blowing away!!)

Sunday April 24th

Dear Folks,

Excuse the stationary, but it's all on hand at the moment. Tonight we are spending in Aden. We'd planned to be in Tel-Aviv by now but there was no load waiting for the plane here today, hence the delay. Aden is only 10° North of the Equator & sure is one _hot_ place. I sat in the Co-Pilot seat on the way down while Herb was flying the plane. It was interesting to look down & trace where we were on the navigator map.

This afternoon we went shopping & bought our first household possession - an electric flatiron. After some bickering with the native dealer, we managed to get one with heat-control dial. It's heavier than those in the States but will be a big help in Tel-Aviv where laundry prices are sky high. We're also going to see about getting an electric plate.

Tonight we're on the roof of the Crescent Hotel with a British immigration officer & his wife listening to Bach played on records. There are tables & chairs placed around the roof & a cool breeze with stars overhead.

I'll see if Herb wants to add anything to this.

XX Tinky

How's Buddy? Give him a kiss from me!

P. S. The immigration chap is named Cartinight. He is a Captain in the Aden Police. The music is passable, the beer is good, the atmosphere excellent. I'm Happy. Herb

(me too!)

Aden is a big shipping port - very rocky country, native & dirty.

The natives are inferior to those at Asmara - guess they resent the British control more.

The C46 at Aden Airport

Aden – "The Garden Spot of The World"!

---

29 June 2006

I rambled on, talking quickly, racing the clock.

"I am struck so much by her use of the word 'natives'. What a different world it was then. To me the word 'native" conjures up grammar school pictures of Native American Indians in head-dresses or Africans in loincloths! But for her it's anyone native to that country. Makes sense when you think of it used that way."

"I have to smile at Dad's scribbled note at the bottom of the page. It's so dad-like. He was a big fan of classical music. Mom played opera and sad love songs a lot. Dad was always playing German beer drinking songs, or Bach and other classical pieces."

"The night sounds so romantic…"

"And they sound so happy."

"Mom's letters seem to shut down a bit over her time there. She never did like to look at the bad or upsetting things in life and I think it got harder for her as time went on to be over there."

"Already? It seems like I just got here!"

"Ok; see you next week."

"Oh…yeah…that's right…4th of July is a Tues…OK on the 6th… sigh."

I felt both sad and lost, and angry at myself for running away from what was inside of me. The room seemed dark and claustrophobic. I stood up, wanting to run away, but knowing that I'd carry it all with me. My therapist held up her notepad and gave me that knowing look. I answered her unspoken question.

"Yes, I'll do some writing…"

---

4 July 2006 – 6pm

Happy 4th of July. I would call my mother on every holiday…I called her every Sunday for a lot of years. Called her every day the last year of her life…well, almost every day. Sometimes I needed a break. And sometimes she couldn't hear her phone. Or maybe sometimes she needed a break.

The 4th of July was my grandfather's birthday. He used to say he was a Yankee Doodle Dandy – born on the 4th of July! We'd all go down to Grampa's house in New Bedford: the three of us, and the 5 cousins with my uncle and aunt. My Great Aunt Allie would make Grampa's favorite dish: swordfish. She'd make lots of carrots (for me cause they were my favorite vegetable!) and then a bunch of mashed potatoes. The cousins would eat like there was no tomorrow! Cousin Dwight had a hollow leg! He'd pack away 5-6 helpings. I'd try to keep up but usually got full after seconds. And then there were the brownies for dessert. I guess there was some sort of cake for Grampa. Probably yellow cake with mocha frosting. I know she used to make him tapioca pudding cause he liked it a lot.

Mom ate a lot of tapioca pudding last year. It was one of the things I knew she'd eat so I bought her a bunch every time I went down to visit...

Today doesn't seem like the 4th of July. It never has been my favorite holiday anyway, even when we'd visit Cottage St (Grampa's) with the cousins. The cousins would always try and play marbles and steal your marbles. I didn't like playing that way. And I couldn't really relate to them. Plus I was probably a tad bit jealous that they took up Allie's time and attention.

I loved it when Allie used to take me on a tour of the old house though! It was an amazing place. Mom said they had servants when she was small. There were the old servants' quarters in the back. You could get to it up the back stairway or through the closet! That was a magical thing to me. And then the buzzers all used to work. They finally disconnected them after we children drove them crazy buzzing away! But the panel in the butler's pantry was neat – with all the rooms indicated to show who had buzzed. There was even a buzzer under the dining room table! Even the attic had a number of rooms to it! And then there was the widow's walk with the colored windows. It was only the bottom half that had colored glass in it but that was the only half I could see out of so it was another magical place.

Grampa's office was a forbidden place. I think I got spanked for exploring in there once. It had two entrances – one was off of the hallway where there was a sink and this lovely rose water and glycerin hand lotion that Grampa used to make himself. Mom used to sneak some every time we visited. The other was from a parlor, which had an entrance to the outside for the patients.

The basement was huge. There were two furnaces. One of which had never been converted to oil so Allie would let us reach in and dig out a piece of coal to make coal plants with.

The place was huge. Imagine growing up in it with servants; with a houseful of people living there, and then living in a tenement and coming to visit with two children at your heels. And there was room there for us all. But mom had been kicked out, according to my step-mom. In hindsight, that may have been true. Interesting that she had to guiltily sneak a squirt of hand-cream.

I will never know for sure what happened…

So happy birthday, Grampa – I haven't thought of you in years.

April 1949 – Saturday

Saturday April

Dear Folks,

It's hard to keep track of the days - they run into each other. But I know today is Saturday for it's the Sabbath here & all shops are closed. Herb left this morning on a flight to Nicosa for gas, then to Aden to pick up a load of passengers to bring here to Tel-Aviv. He'll probably be back tomorrow evening, but things never go on schedule in the flight game. It is an odd life, and quite a radical change for me. Can you imagine spending a honeymoon with 7-8 pilots & radio operators, etc., constantly dropping in to sit on the bed & chat? It will take me a while to get used to it & this constant moving. We spent

the first of our two nights & one day back in Tel-
Aviv at a lovely new hotel - the Sharon - about
20-30 miles out from town. We had the bridal
suite, & food & service were excellent. The hotel is
right overlooking the Mediterranean - a beautiful location. Now we're back at the Garden -
moved in here yesterday afternoon. Tomorrow
we'll have a room of our own, but for the present
we're in one that is full of the baggage & clothes
of the two men who had it before, & they have
to keep coming in to dress or get their things.
Yesterday I walked in on one in his underwear,
but I guess you have to get used to things like
that! I'll be glad when we have our own room &
can find things for a change!

My wisdom tooth kicked up yesterday, so Herb
took me to a Jewish dentist here. He gave me

something to quiet it & another appointment for this morning. It's fine now, but he advised me to have it out when we get Stateside. My cold probably provoked the trouble. The 54 I came here on is scheduled to return to the States tomorrow, & the fellow are pretty glad about that. Herb's plane - the 46 - is due for return May 20th, but they may get an extension on its stay here as there are more Adenites in the offing to be transported. That would prob-ably mean 2-3 months further work, but as I say - you can't count on any- thing & never know what will turn up next. The Maguires will be staying here with us, I think, as well as the double crew for the 46, while Herb took a nap yesterday afternoon, Ted Sturn, radio operator - took me on a tour of Tel-Aviv

Ted Stern (radio op.)
art Ford (co-pilot)
Herb (capt.)

6 Jul 2006

I took the letter back from my therapist. I tried to reconcile in my mind the woman overseas, moving from hotel to hotel, to the one I knew who never wanted to leave her home. The letter spoke to me of a woman who was growing and expanding into her world around her. Random thoughts flitted through my brain and out my mouth:

"I would have thought mom would have been in her element around so many men."

"I guess it would have been tough to keep track of the days without a regular schedule."

"I remember near the end she used to be proud that she knew what day it was."

"I could always call her and get a weather report for the week!"

I felt like I had been stabbed in the chest, as the thought that I could never call her again popped into my head. She was always there at the other end of the line, always willing to listen. I reached out for the Kleenex box through a blur of tears.

"Thanks for the Kleenex."

"Whew – when it hits, it hits...the sadness...missing her...it just comes out of the blue..."

I thought of how smart she was. She always had advice for me when I called, whether it be helping calm me down when I lost the kittens (who came out when they were hungry, just as she said!), telling me how to cook the turkey (salting the cavity before stuffing it), pruning the lilacs (right after they finished flowering), or replacing a light switch (turn off the electricity first). And she always asked how I was doing and cared when I was sick.

"Oh, I hurt so much."

"I need the wastebasket."

"Thanks."

"It's so hard to accept that she's gone."

"Can I read another letter?"

I opened another envelope and pulled out the tissue paper thin airmail paper with the familiar handwriting penned on it. I unfolded the letter and started reading it aloud.

8 May 1949

May 8ᵗʰ

Dear Mom & Dad,

Tonight Herb & I felt like plutocrats, when Sam Cohen came back from the flight with 13 letters for us - 5 from mother, 2 from Mary-Lou, 2 from Frances Congdon, 2 from Mr. Macy, 1 from Aunt Allie, & 1 from Aunt Alice Macy. Besides which a letter came to the Yarden from mother yesterday. We reveled in all our mail & had just time to read through it before Herb left for the field. He left at midnight, & since it's now 1 A.M. - that makes it May 9ᵗʰ! We did so enjoy your letters & had a wonderful time reading them together. Thanks for sending the wedding announcement card, we both liked the simplicity of it. I'll bet that starts a lot of people looking up Eritrea on the map. I'll write Mary-Lou, but you might thank her for the clipping, though Herb says he's got a score to settle with A.A. for putting him as director of special operations. He says "Some operations, with one C-46!" - & I'm to hide the clipping from the other fellows as they won't razz him - & they sure would! I was quite upset to hear about Bill's bout with Chickenpox. That's an awful shame - how the heck did he get it! We hope both he & little Billy are well by now & also that Sylvia is over her sickness. I'm glad Bill could get an extension on his thesis.

It sounds as if you've had quite a bit going on at home. Give Buddy a kiss & tell him to stop eating so much junk & getting sick.

I've been struggling to put a little weight on Herb & think I'm finally succeeding. He gets lots of sleep these days he has off, & I never saw anyone so appreciative of having a "home" & so proud of it. The fellows come in at all hors & say "how about a cup of coffee?" - & this morning I served coffee to six at once, which of course crowded the room somewhat, but it's fun to entertain in our home & pleases Herb so. Then I usually get crackers or pastry & serve coffee again in the late afternoon, at which rate we've used 4 jars of Nescafe in one week, but as long as the supply on the C46 holds out that's alright!

This afternoon, which Herb worked on some log sheets, Mrs. Maguire & I went to the beach with a British Major & his wife from South Africa who are hoping for a ride to the States with us. It's as warm here now as midsummer at home & the water feels heavenly. Am getting quite a tan.

I wrote Allie about the lovely jacket Herb had ordered for me from Hong Kong, but neglected to mention that he also got me a matching pair of embroidered sandals - they're darling.

I waved Herb & the rest of the crew goodbye from the balcony at midnight & he said he hoped I'd be good & lonesome & I will be - but it's surprising how much laundry collects while he's home, & I've a lot to do tomorrow if Mrs. Maguire & I are planning on visiting Jerusalem & so to bed.

Loads of love to all - we loved your letters,

Herb and Beth   XX

Love to Buddy, Widgie & Beep

   XX   X   X

We've decided to ignore the Macy, Sr. situation & enjoy the time we have together here. I have written them from here & from Asmara. I can't get too much enthusiasm into a letter to them, but an account of our doings. It bothers Herb that his father has taken the attitude he has, but it is Herb's suggestion that we'd best just go our own way for a while as far as his folks are concerned. I write them because I think they should have some word from their son & his wife.

From the window of our room, looking over the New City. Jerusalem

Jerusalem May 49

---

6 July 2006

I stopped reading and looked up.

"This letter has so much in it! I wish she had spoken to me about these letters and how she felt being overseas and getting news about sickness delivered to you from home far away. We could have connected. I can relate so much from having been stationed in Wales and reading letters from home there and writing back. There was another missed opportunity for me to have learned more and for us to have formed a deeper relationship."

I had a vision of mom standing in her kitchen, eating her chopped up salad and cottage cheese.

"I can't imagine mom trying to put weight on!"

I had to continue my show and tell and passed three pictures over to my therapist.

"I found more pictures too. Aren't they neat? What cramped quarters inside that plane!"

The C-46 instrument panel

Inside the plane - prostrate with the heat - about 125°; That's the bag that was given one in Asmara.

"Time's up? It goes so quickly. Time goes far too quickly..."

7 July 2006

I feel empty inside
I crave
I seek to fill the void
I buy, eat, run around...
But nothing works
I feel
So all alone.

10 July 2006 - midnight

You know as I am going through these letters I'm remembering more of my mother. She loved animals and nature. She always was taking in stray cats – that's one thing she and my dad had in common. He once had 15 cats! She had 6 at the most. She loved cats. And she loved birds. It was always hard on her when the cat would bring home a trophy and leave it by the washing machine in the cellar.

I hear the birds now
They sing directly to me
I think that they are
in some way
a connection
to those who have passed
At least
in some way
it gives me comfort
to think that way

The mind goes round and round
Not stopping
not resting.
I want the pain to go away
But then,
what will be left?

I fought her
I loved her
I hated her
But at least
it was life.
Death
is so final
leaving nothing behind
except imperfect memories
and an aching want
a need to go back in time
to grasp once more
what one has lost
forever

She was so strong
and yet so weak…
she was
a human…
She claimed she'd live 'til 90
and died at 83
She wrote:

"It is my
intention
to live in spirit
I am going
to live

in spirit"
Are you, mom?

There is so much inside
I think I will burst.

---

10 July 2006 – 6:30am

They say the veil
between two worlds
is thinnest in the early hours
of the morn
Perhaps it is that
or perhaps
the pull of the full moon
on the earthly body...
I scream inside

Losses.
Each one
leaving an emptier world
but also
giving an opportunity
to reach inside
to find
the real meaning
of your own existence

Is it Gods way
of making you wake up?
Of giving you
yet another chance
to look around
and grasp fully
the world
that has been given
to you

It is the cycle
of life
or,
of death -
a continuity
that ensures change
that forces awareness
if
you will listen

Tender hearted
touch a nettle…
There is always a choice:
run hide
busy busy busy
or
find another way
life is too short

11 July 2006

I sat down heavily on my therapist's couch and sighed. I handed her my writings for us to discuss later. I scratched my head trying to think of what to say first. My therapist smiled and asked me how my 4th of July was.

"Did I have a good 4th of July? I guess so. I never do anything much on the 4th. "

In my mind I could see a vision of sitting with my mother and my nephew by the waterfront in Newburyport, having staked out good seats for over an hour.

"I once invited mom and my nephew up for the 4th and they got so scared by the fireworks we had to go home."

I remembered them cowering from the noise and asking to leave and my surprise at their reaction and bitterness at having to leave.

"Took me a long time to stake out those good seats too."

I remembered the party I held the next day where they hid together in the back room until everyone had gone home. But mom had shown me how to make the dips look pretty the night before. I was so surprised that she knew how to entertain. And then she wouldn't socialize. It just hadn't added up. And this didn't jive with the person overseas entertaining the crew with Nescafe! I felt like I had failed to get to know her somehow.

"I feel empty inside. And then there's sadness and longing underneath that starts to surface. I miss her so much. How can you miss someone you never really knew?"

My therapist commented that I looked tired. I tried to sit up straighter.

"I'm not sleeping well yet. But I get up and write when I can't sleep. I'm so tired. I don't have energy for anything! It's hard to keep up with the rest of life…"

I felt my throat start to close and my nose start to fill. I was so very tired of tears. I started talking to distract myself from the feelings inside.

"You've rearranged the table. It's harder to get the Kleenex box."

"What? Oh – I just don't know what to think any more. I'm tired."

""I have another letter. I am finding more pictures too. A strange format – tiny little things."

"Yeah – I could bring them in sometime…I may have one here with me."

"I just don't know what to say or how I feel. Perhaps if I read some more?"

---

24 June 1949 – Kowloon – Hong Kong

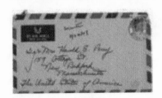

June 24th

Dear Folks,

Pouring rain today - & it really comes down in sheets here. Herb & I have just been out to see about furniture for our future home in Everett. We visited the factory where they make hand-carved teak wood chests, etc., & are having a chest & desk shipped to Everett to be there for us when we come home to start settling down. The safest place we can think of for them to send the bill of ladling is to you for father to put it in the safe for us. Someday we'll have a nice home of our own & that's something we're both looking forward to & planning for now. We also got a round coffee table with cherry-wood insert too - just wait till you come down to visit us; we'll have a most unusually-furnished house. After living in hotels we'll just appreciate our own home.

Maguire hasn't come back yet probably because of the bad weather. I doubt if we'll be leaving Sunday, anyway, since there's so *much to be done on the C46. Meanwhile, we're getting a good rest after the trip over & thoroughly enjoying the change from Tel-Aviv austerity meals. It's good to get milk again - & pasteurized, too.*

More later & lots of love to all,

X Tinky X

---

11 July 2006

"And I found a picture of the plane in Hong Kong. 'Tricky airport'! I would say so!"

I remembered standing, beneath the shadow of the tenement in our tiny back yard at 85 Armour St with mom listening to a plane flying far overhead, and being so impressed when she said what type of plane it sounded like. I could see those fluffy clouds overhead and hear the rumble of the engines above them and wondered how she knew so much about planes.

"Funny I remember mom being adamant about 'never flying on a single engine plane'. Now I can finally understand where she was coming from. This one was small enough but at least you had an engine when one conked out! They must have had a number of close calls that she never talked about. Dad was like that too. He'd just say – 'I took the plane from point A to point B.'"

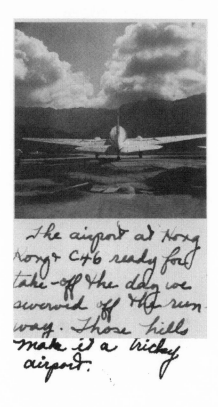

The airport at Hong Kong & C46 ready for take-off the day we swerved off the run way. Those hills make it a tricky airport.

My mind went to our home at Armour St and I mentally inventoried the rooms and the cupboards. I only remember two small teak statues of bent over Oriental men that I used to polish with furniture polish until they glowed. One even had tiny white teeth.

"My step-mom says mom sold all the furniture. Too bad it sounds lovely. She apparently sold a lot of stuff. She even sold Allie's china but Allie made her buy it back."

I wondered silently if that was the rift that forced mom out of her father's house and into her own apartment with us kids. I always resented that grandpa had so much empty space in that huge whaling house in New Bedford. I focused on the letter and started speaking quickly.

"I never knew they lived in Everett! That's a surprise…"

"Her letters say 'Dear Folks' but it sounds like she's really writing to her mom. I really don't know what her relationship was with her folks. She wrote them a lot. I think she was lonely. Funny, huh, with all those people around?"

"Perhaps they never lived in Everett. It doesn't really say they definitely have a home there. But where are they shipping this stuff?"

"She speaks a lot about food. Amazing for someone who ate so little."

"I wish she'd say more about the flights."

I paused long enough to make eye contact with my therapist and for her to tell me to breathe.

"How do I feel?"

First silence filled the room and then sobs. I tried to talk in between nose blows.

"The Kleenex is still too far away."

"Her folks used to call her Tinky Loo. Funny, that, hey?"

"What? I don't know. Tired, I guess."

I opened another letter.

31 May 1949

(Am looking forward to seeing Hong Kong. By the time we get back to New England I'll have been around the world, provided we go home via Hong Kong!)

Dear Folks,

I think today is Thursday & I think it's the 31st. Right now I'm in the plane & we're flying down the Red Sea to Aden. Just looked on the map, & we're over Abu Madd - 3 hours out from Lyddya, 5 hours to Aden. I found 7 or 8 letters on the plane that I'd given the fellows to mail on the last couple of trips. You'd have them now if I'd mailed them in Tel Aviv, but I was trying to dodge the censorship!

We're staying over tonight in Aden, there tomorrow to pick up a load at Djibouti, & should be back in Tel-Aviv tomorrow night | air pocket - makes writing hard!) Maguire hasn't come back from Hong Kong yet, but this flight will finish up Aden. Then two more trips to Asmara, & we'll be ready to go to Hong Kong.. There'll probably be work there for the 46 for a couple of months. Then by the end of that time there'll be a lot more Yemenites in Aden ready to be flown to Tel-Aviv, & I think we'll be in on the job. How long a project that'll be, I don't know. There are enough to keep a C46 busy for a year over here. But this C46 is leased from the U.S. Government, & the lease expires Sept. 30th. Whether we'll have to bring the plane back then or whether they can renew the lease & keep it here is something I know nothing about. I try to give you some inkling of what our plans for the future are,

but they change so constantly that I can never
be sure for long.

When we reach Hong Kong, Ted Sturn our
radio operator is going to the States. He'll land
there on the West Coast, of course, but is planning to eventually get to New England. I've told
him to look you up & plan to stay overnight in
New Bedford. He was at our wedding, & he's a
grand person - so make him welcome as you
always do! I had an awful twinge of longing
to see you when I found out we weren't going
home on the 20th. In fact I was darned homesick for a few days - that's when I had what the
doctor called a gall bladder, but I think it was
mainly food poisoning, as I ran a fever & had
cold chills. But my home is wherever Herb goes
& I won't think too much about the States till
I know we're definitely on our way! Though I

was trying yesterday to remember an American meal & what the food tasted like in the States - but gave up!

It's good to be flying again - I've missed it.

Herb has been waiting around in Tel-Aviv for Maguire to come in.. The natives around these parts do beautiful work in silver, & while we were in Jerusalem Herb bought me a lovely silver necklace & matching earrings with turquoise colored stones & a wide silver link bracelet that has the twelve signs of the zodiac on it. Mr. Schweide, who's head of the American Joint Jewish Commission at Tel-Aviv took us over Jerusalem & showed us the ruins of recent fighting. There wasn't a window left intact in Jerusalem after the war. The buildings are all shrapnel & bullet scarred, & there are two bullet holes in our bedroom walls at the hotel, plus a shattered pane & hole where one bullet entered the window. Of course the Arabs still hold the Holy City so we couldn't go in there. From the distance we could see the red fezzes of the Arab guards as they paced the wall. You can get into the Old City if you go with a United Nations member when they happen to be going, but it would be risky business for any~~member~~one associated with Alaska Airlines! The Jews fought a stiff battle here, & you've got to hand it to them for their courage & tenacity. After seeing the scars of the battle in Jerusalem, I didn't object so much to their new Austerity Program that's been imposed here. Under the Austerity Program, food servings are smaller & you can have no seconds or special menus in the restaurant. Prices for meals are lower, but it costs you more in the long run. To get enough to eat, we go to a second restaurant

& start right in again! Prices are exorbitant in Palestine. Our two nights at the Eden Hotel in Jerusalem cost us 20 pounds or $60.00. But we figured it as a health investment & cheaper than a trip to a hospital as it put my stomach to rights again, the food being good, ample, & <u>clean</u>. The country around Jerusalem is lovely compared with Tel-Aviv, & the quiet nights for sleeping & fresh cool air made us feel as if we'd been on a week's vacation. It's a two-hour drive there from Tel-Aviv over a "road" that's more shell holes than road. Mr. Simon, from Aden, took the trip with us & suggested a cab home instead of the bus, & boy how that rickety old car took those bumps! I took quite a few pictures in Jerusalem & of ruined Arab villages from the bus on the way over. They're being developed now & I'll send them over to you when they're done.

We've brought our suits along to go swimming in Aden tonight. I do love that night swimming under the stars.

There's been no mail from New Bedford for ages. I've wondered how Bill's graduation went & think of you all often.

The first thing we do when we get to the Crescent Hotel in Aden is to order a big steak! The food there is good. It's going to be hot, too - that heat is indescribable! You know, I spent one night a week or so ago dreaming of an American ice cream I'd like & couldn't get beyond vanilla! Isn't that the darndest way to spend a night! It's not that I'm starving to death - just an American trying to get used to foreign food - believe me, there's nothing like the American way of life - though I do think they could incorporate a few ideas from other countries - like the wine with meals & fruit for dessert!

Now for a nap to pass the time. Blackie isn't co-pilot this trip, Redlinger is - a man left behind from the C54 - & he's too big a guy to keep asking him to crawl out of the co-pilot seat to let me ride there! You have to step up and over & then jump down. Plus that & manipulating the tiny rung ladder to board the plane, I'm getting quite athletic, though I've yet to go crawling out the window onto the wings! Loads of love to all.

XX Tinky

Looking from a roof-top over Jerusalem. The old city by sheytr tower in background.

War-scarred street in Jerusalem.

11 July 2006

I kept the letter and the pictures on my lap while I talked to my therapist.

"Did I tell you that she broke all of Allie's china after she bought it back? Of course I don't know that for sure but I heard that she did that."

I thought of mom losing her tempter and hitting us with the fly swatter.

"Yeah she had a fierce temper. She used to drag us around by our hair when she got angry."

"Oh, I did tell you that before.... Ha – you know, the kids in the neighborhood were all scared of her. She made us tow the line!"

I inwardly flinched and closed my eyes as young Heather in my mind ran from her mother and her sister and hid in the bathroom. I could feel the pressure of the bathroom door against my back, the claw foot of the tub against my foot, and my leg buckling as it tried to hold back both mom and Deb battering down the door to drag me out. I opened my eyes again.

"I wonder what her relationship was like with her folks."

I had a picture of Grampa in my mind: his black hair slicked back, the small glasses framing a stern expression.

"Grampa scared me. He was a very stern man. But my sister remembers him as very loving and rocking her to sleep every night when we lived there. I was too young. They tell me that he tried to give me a sedative to make me go to sleep and I ran around the room all night until it wore off."

A vision floated by of being small, sitting on the toilet, Grampa yelling at me to use only two pieces of toilet paper, scared that he'd come in and check each time I went…

"Yes I was always the stubborn one."

In my mind I heard mom's voice floating over the tenements, yelling at me to come home, and my feet hitting the pavement as fast as they could to beat the echo home before I was in trouble.

"Her letters sound so calm and in control. That amazes me."

I pulled out a printout and held it in my lap with the letter.

"I'm still searching on the web for information about Operation Magic Carpet. There's a lot less information than I expected to find. The best is on Alaska Air's site, but it gives a one-sided view. I'd like to get more different views so I can try to find what may be the reality in the middle of all the views. This article talks about both Maguire and Wooten."

Challenges and Inspiration[16]

Two former Magic Carpet pilots recall challenges, dangers and inspirations.

Stanley Epstein says he is not a religious man, but Operation Magic Carpet "had to have been blessed by God because the possibility of any of these airplanes being successful was pretty remote."

Epstein, a pilot and maintenance specialist, was airlifting supplies from Czechoslovakia to Israel. When that operation ended, he contracted with Alaska Airlines to help with Operation Magic Carpet. The humanitarian airlift operation brought more than 40,000 Yemenite Jews to Israel between late 1948 and early 1950.

"Their legend said they would be returned to Israel on the wings of an eagle. Alaska Airlines painted an eagle with outstretched wings over the door of each airplane and it reassured people when they got on the plane. They were living their legend and Alaska Airlines helped fulfill that legend," Epstein said in a phone interview from his home in Los Angeles.

"We flew almost continuously from Christmas Eve 1948 to nearly a year later and never lost a life or had an injury from an accident," Epstein said. "One airplane undershot the runway in Asmara, but it didn't burn, even though it was loaded with gasoline barrels. We had a few bullet holes. But only one airplane had to land in hostile territory when it ran out of fuel and landed in Port Sudan (Egypt). The pilot (Bob Maguire) told the airport officials he needed ambulances right away to take his sick passengers to the

---

16 http://www.alaskaair.com/www2/company/History/CarpetPilots.asp

hospital. They asked why and he told them the passengers had smallpox. They wanted him out of there right away so he got some fuel and left."

The threat was that Jewish refugees and maybe even crew members would be killed if they landed in Arab territory.

"There was an overpowering humanitarian need," Epstein said. "There was rioting in Yemen over the concentration of Jews. The British - who controlled Aden as a colony - were putting pressure on us to get the airplanes turned around and get the refugees out of there."

Maguire, an Alaska Airlines pilot with management experience, was sent to the Middle East near the end of 1948 by company President James Wooten to start-up Alaska's participation in Operation Magic Carpet.

"I had just come back from the Orient where we had started a charter operation with the government to take civilians into Japan," Maguire said. "I had worked with Jim and had business experience that the other pilots didn't. The combination of business and flying experience was the reason I was asked to start Operation Magic Carpet."

Originally, the operation used only Alaska Airlines planes and crews. But because the demand was so great, additional pilots - such as Epstein - and planes were brought on.

"There were high death tolls in the refugee camps and they were having trouble with the Arabs," Maguire said in a recent phone interview from his home in Ventura, California. "Moving that many people under those conditions required an operation that would have been illegal under U.S. aviation rules."

Epstein noted that C-46 aircraft were carrying 76 passengers per trip - nearly 30 more than licensed for based on the average passenger weight and the number of aircraft exits. And the DC-4s, licensed to carry 60 passengers, was instead flying with 150 Yemenite Jews.

"People from our government came over and saw that this was an emergency situation and allowed us to set up an operation that would move the people," Maguire said.

In addition, pilots flew much longer than would have been allowed in the U.S. Maintenance was difficult and planes flew well beyond their scheduled service intervals, Maguire said. "But remember, the environment was tense and time was of the essence."

"I was flying between 270 and 300 hours a month," Maguire said. "I wouldn't have been able to fly more than 90 hours a month back home. And fuel was a big problem. Israel didn't have enough. We had to buy it from the British in Asmara. We would fill up there with enough to go pick up our passengers in Aden, fly them to Israel and then return."

While the operation was successful it took a toll on Maguire. "I lost my pilot's license a year and a half after I returned because of health reasons," he said. "The doctor was an old friend of mine, a flight surgeon. He told me that he couldn't let me fly any more because of the health and safety issues. I had a heart condition and I didn't find out until later that there were parasites in the water where we swam in Aden that contributed to the problem. That's where the problem started."

Epstein said the danger and logistical hurdles that had to be overcome were top of mind at every turn. But the plight of the Jews is what drove everyone to keep going forward. "For the English-speaking volunteers in Israel, the story of the Jews from Yemen was just another amazing story of the gathering of the Jewish people in their homeland. If there was a single reason felt by all of the English-speaking flight crews and other volunteers, it was a feeling of 'never again' after the press and other news media dramatically revealed the stories of the Holocaust."

11 July 2006

My finger rested near the bottom of the printout. I quickly glanced at the clock, hoping my therapist hadn't noticed me doing that. There were only a few minutes left. I kept my eyes on the printout and started talking quickly to fit it all in:

"Parasites in the water where they swam in Aden! Wow! I wonder if they had any effect on Dad and mom's health in later life?"

"Why couldn't she have shared some of this history with us! This was history in the making and my folks were in the midst of it!"

"Did you know she went to Skidmore?"

"She was a debutant too. A doctor's daughter. Very blue blood. She even had servants growing up. Living in a tenement in New Bedford must have been a shock to her."

My therapist gently touched me on the knee, causing me to look up and realize that she had asked me a question.

"What? Oh, I feel…Angry."

I took a deep breath and slowed down for a moment to see what else I felt.

"Sad too…"

The anger came back, kicking away slowness and replacing it with agitation.

"'It's good to be flying again – I've missed it.' – Who is THAT woman?!! You know I would have liked to have met her. I'm liking her…"

Sadness crawled back inside of me under the anger and forced it back. I reached for the tissues.

"I see you've put the Kleenex box on the couch. Thank you."

"Time's up? Sigh. OK. I'll see you next week."

I paused at the door and turned back towards my therapist. Heartfelt, sincere words popped out of my mouth.

"Thank you."

I quickly walked away.

13 July 2006

"I found another telegram, plus another letter."

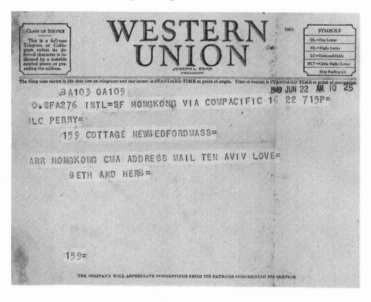

23 June 1949

Room 102

Peninsula Hotel

Hong Kong

June 23rd

Dear Mom & Dad,

Your letter mailed June 15th reached us at the hotel today, & it sure was good to get it!! I think some mail from you must have been lost, since we didn't get any telling about Silvia & Bill's baby being born. Anyway, it was wonderful to get all the news, & thanks for sending the list of wedding presents. I didn't know we had so many! Will write thank-yous from here. I'm glad to hear dad has trained Buddy - more power to him. How'd he do it!

We arrived at Hong Kong yesterday after-noon. It was an easy trip here because we stopped over each night. On the 21st in Bangkok, Siam, & that's a lovely place. The Siamese are very friendly & clean - just the opposite of what we found in Calcutta. The countryside is lovely around Bangkok - very green & lots of streams with pink pond lilies growing. They have bicy-cle-driven rickshaws & we all took rides in them (you can get two people in each) & visited a Siamese nightclub. Calcutta, where we spent the night of the 20th, was a dirty, hot seaport city. We stayed at the best hotel in town - with the lizards slithering around the room & dropping from the walk - plumbing from the year 1 - & heat, whew! We got about two hours sleep that night & were all darned glad to leave! The Indians can have India, but Herb & I wouldn't mind going back to

Bangkok. They have beautiful silver work there & Herb bought me a beautiful pair of pendant earrings & cigarette lighter. They match the bracelet that pilot gave me awhile back in Tel-Aviv. Incidentally MacDonald is now working for Alaska - you remember his wife - that bag who came to visit us - & he came through to Tel-Aviv the same day Wooten did. He gave me a wedding present of compact & bracelet in the same silver work.

Today Herb & I looked around Hong Kong for a birthday present for father but didn't see anything we liked as well as those cigarette lighters in Bangkok. So if you'll please excuse its being a bit late, we're going to pick one up on the way back & ship it home. It won't arrive in time for the 4th but many, many happy returns, happy birthday & lots of love from your two wandering children in the Far East, dad, & we'll be thinking of you July 4th.

Maguire is in ~~Hong Kon~~ Tokyo at present, but due back here any day. Meanwhile there's maintenance being done on the plane & we're taking advantage of the low prices here to have some suits made up. The most beautiful gabardine material - man's suit hand-tailored for $35.00 & woman's for $30.00. Herb is having a dark gray & a navy suit & a Harris tweed sports jacket made up. I'm having a light gray & a navy suit & a camel's hair sports coat made.

You just sketch out for the tailors or tell them what style you want - & they have it all ready for a basted fitting the next day. While we're here we're taking the opportunity to get the suits - think what that would cost at home!

Hong Kong is very nice - wish we could be based here. The food is delicious, & you can get <u>milk</u>, as well as nice thick steaks. We'll probably be leaving here Sunday morning. The rains are on in this part of the world, & every now & then it <u>pours</u>. More later.

Loads & loads of love to all,

X Tinky X

---

13 July 2006

I was back in the therapist's office, sitting on the couch with my shoes kicked off and my feet up on the footstool. I had placed the telegram and letter on the couch next to me. I gently touched them with a fingertip.

"It still strikes me whenever I open a letter and see her handwriting. I usually have to pause a moment after taking one out of the envelop. I hold the tissue paper thin airmail paper in my hands and feel like I'm opening an historic scroll. There is suspense as I start to read the words. The handwriting looks just like what she would write on a card or letter to me. And I simultaneously smile and cry - It brings me so close to her. Then I get drawn into the letter and the world around me disappears for awhile with mom's world of 1949 opening up around me like a movie starting in a darkened movie theater. And then I get to the end of the letter and it's that same feeling shock of having the movie lights turned up at the end of a particularly engrossing movie and having to leave the theater and return home to reality. And the truth is that this feeling of being close to her is a passing artifact, much like the fantasy of the movies."

"Yes I do need the Kleenex, thanks."

I took the rectangular cardboard box from my therapist and noted that it was full. As I wiped my eyes and blew my nose I wondered if she had a stock of Kleenex in the closet.

"No matter how much she is still here with me in my memories, it will never be the same as having her here in person. And we'll never relate to each other the way I wanted us to."

I balled up more Kleenexes on the couch on the other side of me away from the letter.

"Wastebasket? Thanks..."

I looked up at my therapist as I dropped the wad of Kleenexes in the wastebasket.

"I so wish I could have talked to her in person about these places. Especially as I traveled to India and other places she may have passed through."

I reached out and lightly touched the letter again.

"I do have to smile – both Dad & Mom liked to buy clothes. I can see Dad in that Harris Tweed jacket!"

I tenderly put another letter down on the couch cushion. Each letter felt so precious to me.

16 July 1949

ALASKA AIRLINES

AMSTERDAM OFFICE

SCHIPHOL AIRPORT

TEL. AMSTERDAM 38141

July 16ᵗʰ

Dear Folks,

This paper shows you how Alaska Airlines gets around - we've offices all over the world. This morning I was up bright & early, had breakfast at the house here & then set into a big wash - how that stuff does collect! I had to use the bathtub to wash in & then was stumped for a place to hang them to dry. So went up on the roof with a ball of twine & scissors, wrapped the twine four times across two posts, pinned the clothes on with safety pins, & felt quite proud of my inventiveness. It's surprising what you can rig up in a pinch! Then I wrote Frances C., Bill & Sylvia, & Aunt Alice Macy - both Frances & Aunt Alice M. have been wonderful to write so often. Mail means so much.

Then I came across, while sorting through a bunch of papers, the letter in which you told of father receiving Herb's letter. I thought Herb would bust his boiler the night he read that, but he can't tease me any more because now he has pimples on _his_ fanny, too! Though he claims he never had before we were married. Honestly, we do have fun, though Herb is working very hard and gets overtired at times. Then a good head rub or backrub fixes him up.

Household hint: have discovered a marvelous time saver for clothes not dirty enough to wash but spotted or soiled at cuff or collar. A small, stiff nailbrush, dipped in hot water and rubbed over a cake of soap makes an excellent spot-remover.

This is a great boon to me, since we're both fastidious about appearance, and I don't want to spend _all_ my time washing!

Later: -

Am relaxing now with a cup of Nescafe' -& does that taste _good_ - after ironing my wash and cleaning and pressing trousers and dresses. Took a short sunbath on the roof while the wash was drying, & boy was that sun hot! Now to tackle myself with manicure, pedicure and bath, & then to the Yarden to visit the 54 crew and get supper.

Loads of love to all,

X Tinky X

13 July 2006

"Dad always used to say that 'every beautiful woman had a pimple on her fanny'. I didn't understand what he meant at the time! I took it too literally! Years later I got an: 'Aha! That's what he meant!' Now it is funny to see mom use the same expression. It ties them together in my mind in some way."

I thought of Dad's expressions: 'He died with his boots on'; 'Put your nose to the grindstone, your thumb halfway to your nose and your ear to the ground and if you can do that, you can do anything!' They were both such characters. I tried to imagine them living together.

"Mom hated housework."

I remembered the cat box smell in her house, the piles of bagged junk mail hidden under her kitchen table, the dust balls under the TV stand, the clutter piled everywhere, cat dishes scattered across the floor and kitchen table, the secretary desk so bursting with papers it wouldn't close any more.

"I was thinking what a mess her house was in the end. I don't think she had cleaned it in years."

I stood up, unable to sit any more, knowing that it was time to go any way.

"Next week it is..."

16 July 2006

Unbearably hot...
and yet
I don't feel

The surroundings are meaningless
sometimes.
Sometimes
it is a world that I live in
within
Within me
swirls a world
of pain
hunger
confusion
want
hurt
I feel lost
Lost and searching
for answers
for someone who once was
but is no more.
Someone
myself
my mother
my roots
her past
his past
their past
my past

all swirls together
in one long continuum
A thread from the beginning of time
picking up in 1949
birthing me in 1953
and continuing on
through today
to tomorrow
and beyond
what will it bring?
Peace?
Internal calm?
I only wish I knew
how to find my way
and also
I long just once more
to talk to mom
to Dad
to Allie
And then I move on
to a swirl of activity
but sometimes
Just sometimes
I pause
and remember

2 Aug 1949

Tel-Aviv August 2

Herb left for Aden three days ago and is now stuck there with engine trouble and no parts for repair. So we've been scurrying around trying to get an airlines that makes connections through Asmara and from there by BOAC to get the part to Aden. You see, Alaska is the only line direct from here to Aden. No word yet from Maguire. I got a cable for Herb from Seattle asking for complete expense report on this area, so Ford and I are going to go over the account I've been keeping tonight, since there's no telling how long Herb will be held up in Aden.

It's very lonesome while he's gone, but Mike is great company. He grows more every day, I'm sending a picture we had taken sitting at a Café here in Tel-Aviv with our pooch. I hope you got my cable asking Wilber to airmail the left lens for my glasses in care of American Lloyd, 44 Rothschild Blvd. The left lens fell on the floor and broke. I can get it fitted in here! I miss them!

Please thank Mary-Lou, Sam and Suzy very much for their birthday card and tell Mary-Lou that I'll write as soon as there's news and time

---

18 July 2006

As I walked into my therapist's office I wished I didn't have to be there. I wanted it all to go away. I wanted to be done with it. Done with talking things out. Done with taking the extra time out of my day with driving and the appointment. I wanted life to be normal again. I reached inside of me to get the words that would make it all heal the fastest, to explain what was going on, while knowing that it was just a process that would take its own path, despite my best efforts.

"You know how I said I felt I was living in two worlds? No, I didn't? Well I wrote about it but I was wrong – it's more like three worlds: Now, my past, and 1949!"

I struggled to express the feelings inside – what it was like every day since mom passed away.

"Actually more than that – 'Now' has two different realities too – the reality of sitting here and the reality of making it through every day: work, friends, relationship, dog, cat, ..."

I knew my therapist would pick up on the wording I used, so tried to beat her to it.

"Does it feel like 'making it through'? Somewhat – some days I don't want to be doing what I'm doing at all – I want to crawl back into bed or run away or scream or cry or just do nothing."

I paused and thought of what else expressed the uncontrollable feelings inside.

"Sometimes I do scream in my car going over the bridge. I do cry a lot in my car."

I pulled out of the dark and unknown inside of me and returned to the more familiar and handed my therapist a web page print out.

"I've been doing a lot of research. Trying to fill in around the letters...."

Extracted from: Jewish Emigration from the Yemen 1951-98 (SOAS Centre for Near & Middle Eastern Studies) by Reuben Ahroni

Operation Magic Carpet (also called Operation On Eagles' Wings) came to an end on September 24, 1950. It involved nearly 450 flights, carrying a total of about 50,000 Yemeni Jews to Israel in just two years (1949-1950). In the preceding thirty-eight, only 18000 had emigrated to Israel. [17]

This dramatic air-rescue operation, which was sponsored by the American Joint Distribution Committee (henceforth: AJDC) and paid for by American Jews through the United Jewish Appeal, consisted of three phases. The first phase began on December 17, 1948[6] by the middle of the month, there were no Yemeni Jews left in the Hashed Camp which was situated in the British Colony of Aden, resulting in its closing.[6]

The second phase of Operation Magic Carpet concentrated on the native Jews of Aden. These Jews had just emerged from the devastating pogram of December 1947, in which 82 Jews were killed and 76 Jews were wounded. Faced with economic devastation, destruction of most of their homes, bleak prospects for recovery, and the dashed confidence of the British flag to safeguard their security, most of the Jews of Aden took full advantage of Operation Magic Carpet and left Aden for Israel.[6]

In the meantime, reports began to filter from Yemen that thousands of Yemeni Jews had taken to the roads, striving to reach Aden in the hope of emigrating to Israel. In view of this situation the AJDC renovated the old Hashed camp, expanding its facilities and accommodating capacity. The camp, then renamed 'Camp Ge'ulla' (Redemption), was situated in the desert, a dozen miles from the town of Aden. Aid workers

---

17   Jewish Emigration from the Yemen 1951-98 (SOAS
     Centre for Near & Middle Eastern Studies)
     by Reuben Ahroni

were assigned at certain border posts to meet the refugees and transport them to the new camp. It is to this new camp that the torrents of Yemeni refuges poured and here that the truly spectacular drama of operation Magic Carpet unfolded.[6]

On June 28, 1949, the third phase of Operation Magic Carpet began, concluding on September 24, 1950.[6]

I took the printout back and looked down at it.

"Amazing, isn't it. I wonder if they had any clue they were so much part of history?"

My mind floated to rest on an image of a picture of mom and Dad that I had on my desk at home. In it they were walking hand in hand, mom in a summer dress and Dad in a white shirt and dress pants. Dad looked concerned in the picture, mom looked happy as a lark, without a care in the world.

"My mom definitely didn't seem the type. Dad did – he was dashing."

I smiled with the memory of dad, of his support, of his confidence. A weight in my chest lifted for a moment.

"I found more pictures:"

18 July 2006

"Dad was a handsome man. My sister, Susan, says I look like him! I like that. Mom always said I looked like her, but she never wanted either of us to look like him. My sister, Debbie always thought she looked like Dad but I think she looks much more like mom. I'd like to look like all the best parts of all of them, but more like Dad and Allie. I think I do."

I looked at the picture of Dad with his wild hair and thought how charming he looked. Growing up I often thought he looked a bit like Cary Grant. I could see where I got my uncontrollable hair! After so many years of Dad being gone, memories of him no longer hurt. I hoped it would be like that with mom memories some day.

"I liked Dad's wit so much. He was such a good pilot. So typical that dry 'pessimist" quote!"

"It is interesting to see how much they did with so little support from the States. He was a fantastic pilot. And mom was a very resourceful woman when she wanted to be."

My therapist stopped my reminiscing.

"Time's up, hey? ... OK... there's just so much to wade through here..."

"Can you write down next week's appointment? I know it's the same time but I just like the reminder."

I took the card from her, clutching it like a security blanket.

"Thanks..."

I stood up and walked slowly out the door.

"Bye"

20 July 2006

I ran into the therapist's office, excited to show what I had found.

"Look at the map I found! I wonder when she wrote on it?"

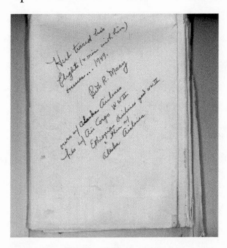

"Look at the area she's talking about in her letters! Just imagine flying that in a small 2 engine plane with people shooting at you!"

I was smiling and happy. Here was a piece from my childhood. The route that mom meant when she mentioned she flew half way around the world with Dad!

I traced the route with my finger.

"When I was growing up, there was no Asmara Eritrea on the maps at school. I used to wonder if mom was lying to me about all of it. Even if they had gotten married at all. Then one day I went to the Christian Science church in Boston. They have a huge globe there that you can walk inside of. It is from that period of time and had Asmara on it! The globe was neat too – if you stand in one side and whisper, a person standing over on the other side can hear the whisper clear as day!"

The excitement of the visit to the globe mingled with that of finding this map. I didn't want to do any therapy that would make me sad so left my writings and terminated the session early.

---

22 July 2006 – 4pm

I dread the day I run out of letters…it'll be like losing a piece of her. I savor reading each one. I see her handwriting and get happy.

I want to call her so much.

17 May 1949 – 8A.M.

Dear folks,

Just a note scribbled before leaving for the field. Laid over here last night because of engine trouble. When we registered at the hotel, they had no rooms left & so fixed a bed for us on the roof - piazza - sleeping under the stars.

Mrs. Simon, Arthur Ford & I took a tour on foot of Crater City yesterday, while Herb was there on business matters. Brother, you've never lived until you've seen these native bazaars & squalor. You feel like taking a bath in Lysol afterwards!

When we got back to the hotel we'd been planning a barbeque on the beach but couldn't get the spareribs. So Ford, Herb & I went swimming at 7:30, & it was lovely with the stars all out & the water phosphorescent so that the bubbles sparkled when you splashed your hands,

Herb bought me a beauty of a camera yesterday, & I've been taking shots like mad ever since. It's a German make with adjustments for light, distance, etc. Also got some Chanel #5 here in Aden, & the price was much cheaper than Italy.

It's hotter than I ever thought it could be. Sweat rolls off you.

So long for now & lots of love,

Tinky X

Inside Crater City

---

23 July 2006 – 9:54 am

What happened to our relationship
you cried plaintively
looking at me through
half blind eyes

You picked Deb I cried
as my two year old

stomped out of the room
and my adult walked me back in

That time sticks with me
I thought of it
as I stared into those eyes
looking for the woman I once knew

Looking for my mom...
I have been for so long
Looking for the strong woman
I called for advice

I was running away from you
when I left to join the Navy
and yet on the way there
I stopped to cry on your shoulder

You were my strength, my guide
the woman who knew so much
yet in the end
seemed to know so little

What happened to our relationship?
we lost that trust
that allows forgiveness
and gives relationships latitude

I grew suspicious
and you grew defensive
and bit by bit it all eroded
but despite it all – we loved.

---

25 July 2006

I drummed my fingers on my thighs and scowled.

"Shouldn't I be done with all of this by now? How long does this process go on?"

I knew the answer and shook my head before my therapist could tell me what both she and I knew. I scowled again and said angrily: "I'm really only beginning it in many ways. Damn. This is painful! I want it to stop!"

I stood up and paced to the window. The tree in the parking lot standing so firm and rooted reassured me. I turned back and sat down again.

"I know, I know…it's a process…and it will get better…"

I shook my head and got ready to continue on.

"Sigh…It's hard to go through all this without going back and looking at Dad's stuff too; I found this in a file I kept with articles on him:"

11 Dec 1984 – The Boston Globe

A life of joy and gusto by David B. Wilson

Herb Macy died last week.

"Was active in civic affairs," said the Globe headline. He would have loved that.

Herb would have grinned, winked and implied that you didn't know the half of it, that not a matron in town remained unravished, that delicious conspiracies were under way, that something terrific was about to happen.

He used to say he wanted to be shot by a jealous husband at 96. He might have made it, but his body wore out, and he died at 65 of too much living.

He was a Macy of that ilk, which is to say, Yankee to the marrow of his bones, like the Folgers and Starbucks of Nantucket and the Baileys, Doanes, Nickersons and Ames of Cape Cod, people who were here before the Revolution and so

have a certain perspective about things.

The Macy line went back to Frederick, an original settler of Nantucket; and, on his mother's side, he was descended from Rebecca Nurse, hanged as a witch in Salem. He was proud of this; but you had to pry it out of him.

The Yankee is supposed to be cold, calculating, shrewd, stingy, taciturn. Herb was the opposite of all that: warm, unpremeditated, impractical, generous, talkative.

Why is any of this important? The obituary has been published, the 'civic affairs,' the member ships, the survivors, right? No, not right, because all of that unspeakably respectable stuff omits rather than describes him.

He was an airline pilot by trade. The obit mentioned that he flew 29 years for American Airlines and, earlier, for Alaska Air-lines and Ethiopian Airlines and, earlier that that, for the Army Air Corps, mostly transports, in World War II. He hated the war and would not talk about it.

The obit did not mention that he gave up trying to figure out how many millions miles he had flown, but estimated that about one-quarter of his waking life had been spent aloft. He was, defying that old aphorism, an old, bold pilot; sitting there out front for all those years without ever crashing a plane or losing a passenger.

Among the things Alaska Airlines did – very quietly – was haul Yemenite Jews from Yemen to Israel in the late 40s and 50s. The Yemini tried to build in-flight cooking fires in the old C46s; and childbirth was common on board. A character in Leon Uris's "Exodus" is modeled after Herb.

With Ethiopian, he flew spear-carrying animist tribesmen and their sheep and goats all around Africa. He flew Moslem pilgrims to and from Mecca.

He drank Scotch on the rocks with a splash of soda, He loved the ladies and he knew his way around Cairo, Tunis, Algiers, Casablanca, Athens, and Rome.

He made a lot of money and probably spent more, quite a bit of it on alimony and child support. His third marriage, to Catherine Reardon, a black Irish beauty from Lawrence, was a stormy but enduring 28-year love affair.

The "civic affairs" part was literally true. He was as responsible as anyone for the restoration and preservation of the 17th-Century Major John Bradford House in Kingston, He served on the Kingston planning board, the conservation commission and the growth and policy commission, reluctantly reconciled to helping a cozy, peaceful, country town get overrun by progress.

He never grew up, never lost that Andy Hardy "let's put on a show" quality. He loved mischief: wherever he was, was where it was at. He was curious about how things worked. He loved fixing up old cars. He sporadically voted Democrat, just to be obstreperous. If he heard you were in trouble, whatever the problem, whether you were right or wrong, he would call up and try to help. He was a very gentle man, a practicing Christian.

Herb graduated from Fairhaven High School. he never finished college, which, in his later years, annoyed him. His father had a little drug store in Plymouth. An ancestor had been fire chief in New Bedford.

Remembering these things is important, I think, because Herb Macy represents a lot of men in a lot of towns in New England and all over this country who live rich, adventurous, useful and important lives but never become famous or powerful and don't mind that. He never had time to mind. He was too intensely engaged in the business of living to care what people thought of him or whether they thought of him at all. When somebody, in the heat of a local political campaign, had a ton of horse manure dumped on his lawn, he thought it excruciatingly funny and spread the manure.

He loved his family, his town, his country and his fellow human beings, without distinction. They are going to miss him terribly.

God knows, I do,

David B. Wilson is a Globe columnist.

25 July 2006

I smiled looking down at that 'piece of Dad' in my lap. A feeling of pride filled my chest. I was his daughter.

"I haven't looked at that column in years. It used to make me cry. Now I remember him fondly. I do miss Dad tremendously. He was such a character. I do believe my parents loved each other very deeply but were just too scatterbrained to be together."

I searched through my memories trying to figure out what mom and Dad were to each other. I had no view of their relationship, and few stories. No wonder I struggled for so many years with my own relationships! I looked up at my therapist and tried to read her face as I tried to make sense of it all. I flipped from snippet to snippet – a collection of unfinished stories.

"Mom used to say Dad would give anyone the shirt off his back. I didn't think she liked that about him though. I think it took the focus off of her. I think at times she must have driven him crazy. Perhaps he drove her crazy too."

"I remember a story that mom tried to put her foot on foreign territory, after Dad & mom had landed to get an engine fixed, and nearly got shot. Seems that the country was barely friendly to them and just wanted to get rid of the plane as quickly as possible. Apparently Dad came running after her and pulled her back up the gangplank, or whatever they had there...I can see her doing that. And him!" I smiled broadly. It felt good to do so.

"Funny – mom did tell the story about the settlers lighting fires in the cabin and scaring her to death that way! I never heard anything about childbirth though! Probably she figured it was too sensitive information for my young ears."

I knew I needed to get at my feelings and was surprised to see that I actually felt good for a change.

"In many ways I am proud of both my parents. Funny mix though with mom for at times I was also so ashamed of her. She was so afraid of life and always tried to look younger than she was. I wanted Mrs. Cleaver not Mrs. Robinson for a mom. "

"I always wondered how I got that job at the Bradford house so easily. I was so proud of being a Pilgrim for a summer! The costume was terribly hot though. How typical of Dad to quietly do something for me in the background and let me be proud of my accomplishment...he was a good man.... I bet though that Kit spurred him on to do it. She was a good motivating force behind him. I think that's why that lasted so long. Kit is practical."

"I remember sitting at the counter at Grandpa Macy's store and getting a free ice cream. I knew he was a pharmacist there but never knew he owned the store!"

"I had two very colorful parents...what a history is here!"

I smiled with my therapist. Perhaps there was a light at the end of the tunnel. I reached in my bag for one more piece of show and tell and drew out a letter from mom.

23 May 1949

Sunday A.M.

Dear Allie,

I wrote to mom & dad yesterday but forgot to date the letter. I think today is the 8th - can't find a camera to make sure. I'm writing this on our balcony overlooking the street & everyone is bustling around & going to work as if it were Monday. It'll be hard to get used to Sunday being Sunday when we get home! We had a lovely leisurely morning at home yesterday. Herb read to me while I shortened the sleeves on his uniform & knitted, then we had lunch "at home" of pea soup, applesauce, cheese, bread, and butter. Later we got some cakes at the little stands that are open on the Shabbath & were luxuriating with coffee in the sun on our balcony when word came through that a 54 was due from Shanghai at 4P.M. Then the fellows descended enmasse! Herb managed to get beds for them & Mrs. Maguire & I cleared out of our rooms so they could shower. This 54 left Tel-Aviv the middle of February for the States & so has circled the world since then. They passed the 54 Maguire is on over Hong Kong & say there's a possibility of that ship being sent direct to the States from Shanghai, which naturally perturbed Mrs. Maguire considerably. In that case, Herb's 46 will have to carry back to the States, as well as its own double crew, the crew from the 54 that were left here & Mrs. Maguire. I know if Bob possibly can make it back to pick up his wife he will, but it's tough on her. I sure would have gone along if Herb had been going away on a week's flight & taken no chances!

Herb had ordered a beautiful pure silk Chinese jacket for me for one of the fellows to pick up in Hong Kong when this 54 left for Tel-Aviv in February, since they knew it was eventually going over there. It's a gorgeous thing – interlined, all hand done, embroidered & in heavenly shades of blue. The same pilot also gave me a box of Jean Patou perfumes – the real stuff – that he'd got in Hong Kong. They're "Amour Amour", "moment Supreme", & "Colony" & smell divine – also a heavy engraved silver bracelet that would be 18-20 dollars in the States. I was overwhelmed – so pressed a suit for him to wear since all his clothes were a wrinkled mess from packing.

Herb bought me a lovely gold cigarette lighter here in Tel-Aviv. He's very thoughtful & a very nice husband. The 46 is due back from

Aden tonight. They were going to stop on the way down at Asmara & while there pick up any mail for us. Then Herb takes it out tomorrow morning, & Mrs. Maguire & I will either take our trip to Jerusalem or spend the time on the beach here, depending on whether or not we can get rooms to stay overnight in the King David Hotel there.

Much love to all - be seeing you soon -

Beth X

---

25 July 2006

The glow of the good feeling remained inside of me. As I traced the letters on the page with my finger I felt a slight familiar pang inside. I looked back up at my therapist.

"Her handwriting is so familiar. It's as if I could reach out and touch her. As if she's still alive."

"Strange that she signed that one 'Beth'. It's so strange that we shared the same name. I felt stamped by it. And tried so hard to make it my own. Now that she's gone I feel a bit guilty about that."

"At the nursing home when I was cleaning out her room, one of the last things I did was to rip my name off the door. It gave me such a shock each time I visited her to see Beth Macy printed there."

"Two people with the same name, and oh so different...."

I paused. The jumbled feeling in my chest was back. I struggled to find where it was coming from.

"She was a Leo, you know? Born 9 August 1922. She never told anyone her age! I had to have it researched for the funeral home arrangements..."

My mind flashed back to standing in the funeral home in front of that casket with the cloying smell of flowers and claustrophobic feeling of finality that I so wanted to flee.

"That was a tough day..."

I sighed and stood up to leave as my therapist rose from her chair.

"We've run over? Sorry..."

She laughed and gently touched my arm. I knew that I didn't need to apologize and smiled.

"OK, not sorry! Thank you."

"See you next week."

I walked out into the sunshine feeling somewhat lighter. I sat in my car in the parking lot feeling the warmth of the late afternoon sun beating down and knew somehow it would be ok. I took a deep breath and started the car and drove slowly out of the parking lot.

26 July 2006 -10am

You can't just
throw away the bad feelings
my therapist said
For it's all entwined: good & bad
When you lose the bad
You lose the good
Was that what happened, mom?
Did you shut away
those parts of you
so painful
so deep
that in doing so
you lost yourself?

27 July 2006 – 2 am

I walk alone
down the path of this journey
we call life
and it scares me

It scares me
because as an elder
it now may very well be
me who is next

It scares me
because
there is still so very much
that is unknown

and most of all
it scares me
because there is no-one
left to guide me

27 July 2006

I ran into my therapist's office, excited at my latest find:

"I found a letter she wrote her father on his birthday. Enclosed was a handwritten menu:"

MENU	#15

No. 1. Fried Prawn

No. 2. Grilled Crab & f. Mushroom

No. 3. Fried egg & Shrimp

No. 4. Steam Red garoup and cream sauce

No. 5. Baked Lobster

"With a note from mom that says:"

'That cost $15. Hong Kong for 4 of us – or about $1.00 U.S. apiece.'

"And a letter that came with it. It's nice to find things that relate to each other and can fill in more pieces!"

4 July 1949

July 4, 1949

Dear Dad,

A very happy birthday to you from Hong Kong. I wish we could be there to help you celebrate, but I'm sending lots of love your way & thinking of you. I couldn't get the cigarette lighter I wanted here, and since we may not be in Bangkok long enough to get it there, we're sending something else. Herb picked out a carved wooden figure that he thinks will look well on your desk, & we're sending that and some ginger to you from Asmara. It will get there quicker.

The heat here is pretty bad now, but we both feel 100% better for the good food & milk we've been having. It looks as if we'll be several more months in Tel-Aviv - 4 at least. Could you please send me (c/0 S.T.A.I.R., Asmara, Eritrea) some more Vitaminetts & Feosol, since I can't get them here & feel we really need them in Tel-Aviv. I'll need some more Proloid, too, if we're staying here 4-6 more months. If they were sent to Tel-Aviv they might be confiscated since they're so funny about the mails there. I don't look forward to rejoining our noisy, Yiddish friends!

Maguire went back to the States on a 54 today, & it's a nice change to have the room to ourselves.

cont'd July 6th

Am enclosing the menu for the Chinese dinner we had on board a boat in Repulse Bay - that on the Island - last night. Freddie & his wife went with us, & it was quite an experience. This afternoon they're test hopping the plane, & we should finally get off by tomorrow noon.

Lots of love,

X Tinky X

---

27 July 2006

"Mom was always a quiet person who enjoyed more 1-1 than group things and loved her solitude. She used to claim she was a people person but she really wasn't. Noise & crowds just weren't her thing. She liked to be rooted in one place. I'm much like her in that way. So I can imagine that here she was, shuttling from place to place, sharing her room with her new husband and these other strangers, in many different foreign lands – well, it just would have been too much for her. She would have been craving quiet and solitude. And must have been very, very, homesick."

"Amazing though – her picking up and following her husband half-way around the world. She was leading an adult life. I think that must have been scary for her."

"Here's another letter:"

---

19 June 1949

June 19th

Bombay

Dear Folks,

It's very hot & muggy here. The monsoon is on now which means the rainy season, lasting from May through October. But so far we've had no rain, just humidity. Everything is very green - so much it almost hurts your eyes, or maybe it's just that we haven't been used to it after Tel-Aviv & Aden.

This afternoon we walked around the Hanging Gardens. They're shrubs there trained to form elephants, giraffes, lions, etc. I took my camera along & got some good shots. Ted, Ford & Tommy got out of quarantine this noon - I guess they had a good rest at the hospital. We leave tomorrow for Calcutta, will spend the night there - the next day at noontime in Bangkok & by night in Hong Kong.

We have a suite at the West End Hotel here - living room, bedroom & bath - very comfortable & with large ceiling fans to keep the rooms cool. We've been having our meals here at the hotel - trying both their Indian & European cooking.

There's much curry in the Indian food, & it burns all the way down!

Loads of love to all -

Tinky X

P.S. Am enclosing map on which Herb has traced our route on the trip - X

---

27 July 2006

I was really excited at the reference to the map and pointed it out to my therapist: "That's it! That's the map I found!!"

"We weren't talking much around the time I went to Calcutta. I wish we could have spoken about it more. I didn't get to see much of Bombay. I know it's changed tremendously from the time she was there though. I do remember telling her about the huge ceiling fans and her remembering them too. It was so nice when-ever we connected. It was so rare."

"How do I feel about that? Sick of feeling. Sick of being sad all the time. Yes angry too."

"Here's another letter. Plus I found another picture of Dad overseas."

"Time to go? Rats...OK... Thanks."

1 July 1949

Dear Folks,

Here are some pictures taken in Bombay, Calcutta & Haifa. There's only one of Calcutta because that's the most unphotogenic place I've struck yet!

The 54 hasn't arrived from Alaska yet, but when it does it's turning right around & going back to the States. So we're sending on it father's birthday present. Herb picked the statue out himself & says it will look good on your desk. I hope the ginger is good, too!

Lot's of love,

X Tinky X

1 August 2006

I walked into my therapist's office with the weight of August on my shoulders. August – "mom's month", August 9th, her birthday. I sat down heavily on the couch, pulled out the latest letter, and started talking.

"I haven't found the rest of the pictures yet."

"She hated Calcutta. I never knew she had been there until I was going there on business and she told me it was the armpit of the world with raw sewage in the streets. I can't wait to find more of her pictures! It would be wonderful to see places I also had been and share that with her."

I sighed and looked down at the letter in my lap, fighting back the tears, escaping into the intellect of it all.

"Going through her letters is fascinating to me – such a picture of the world at that time...of who she was...and it makes me feel that part of her still lives on – a legacy of sorts."

"1949 is an interesting time for the Middle East. From reading *Crisis and Crossfire The United States and the Middle East Since 1945* by Peter L. Hahn, until after WWII, the US largely ignored the area. "

"In light of the Cold War, the United States assigned vast importance to the petroleum resources of the Middle East. The region
boasted the world's largest proven oil reserves, and U.S. officials
considered it vital to deny that resource to Soviet Russia in peace
or war, to use it to fuel the economic reconstruction and revital-
ization of Europe and Japan, and to preserve the Western hemi-
sphere oil reserves for periods of international emergency. In
1947, Arab states supplied half of the oil consumed by U.S. armed
forces and most of that fueling the Marshall Plan. The Central
Intelligence Agency (CIA) deemed Middle East oil 'essential to
the security of the US.' U.S. capital investments in the oil industry,
the State Department added, generated 'substantial revenue' in
federal taxes.[18]

"Not much has changed, hey? Amazing to think of what we're
living through today having started a generation ago."

My therapist placed her hand gently on my knee, her "What am
I feeling?" signal. I looked up at her and said, "I'm feeling sad. It
never really goes away. It's a constant loss deep inside of me. As
time goes by it gets easier to go through the every day motions,
but I can't escape the loss. And I don't expect to. I still cry when
I think of Dad and how much I miss him. And it's August. This is
mom's month."

I took out another letter and smoothed it gently on my knee,
the tissue-like softness of the blue airmail paper rustling under my
touch, and looked up again.

---

18 *Crisis and Crossfire The United States and the Middle
    East Since 1945* by Peter L. Hahn

"She's here. Here in the letters, here inside of me, here in this room. But it's only vignettes that add up to a pale copy of what she was. A shadow figure." I looked back down at the letter.

---

27 April 1949

Dear Folks,

Herb left at 5:00 this morning for the airfield to see about putting some seats in the plane. I've got to be packed when he gets back at 9:00 as well as type a couple of letters for the company - seems none of the fellows here can type so I'm willing to help them out as best I can. Herb is having a couple of seats put up front in the plane, enclosed by a curtain, for me - since the passengers we transport are none too desirable. We're also taking four other Alaska Airlines men with us, as well as the regular crew of, Herb, Blackie, and Ted. They're going to let me co-pilot again this trip - I love to do that! Herb has been with me to the Immigration head here & obtained permission to bring me with him on trips here. We've also had my passport transferred to my married name at the American consulate.

Yesterday we bought an electric kettle to use in our hotel room at Tel-Aviv & help cut down on living expenses there. Prices are sky-high in Tel-Aviv. It's big enough to heat a can of soup inside, boil eggs, etc. Then we looked all over town for bathing suits. I'd left mine in Tel-Aviv & there's a lovely beach & good swimming there. We managed to get Herb a pair of white deck pants, but gave up on the suits & went to the beach with the others just for the sun. You can't take too much of their sun - & the water sure did look good. Next time we'll know enough to bring our suits but had no idea we'd be here so long! The delay was caused by a strike of the passengers we were scheduled to take! They'd been signed up to go for a long time but protested they'd not have time to sell their houses. In Asmara the natives are more like negroes, but here there are Arabs, Indians & Jews, & none of them get along too well together. Naturally it's the Jews we're moving out of here back to the promised land.

After we got back from the beach yesterday, Tom Provans took Blackie, Herb & me on a tour of Crater City - a native settlement near town here. It goes back in time as far as the Egyptian civilization. The city itself is built on the mouth of an extinct volcano &

completely walled in by the mountainous lava piles of ancient volcanic eruptions. (You can reach the city through a tunnel in the mountainside) As a matter of fact all Aden is one rocky pile of old lava heaps, with just occasional groups of trees where there happens to be an underwater spring. Crater City is a most picturesque, typically native villiage[19], smelly, dirty & looking as if it were just waiting for a good big epidemic to sweep through. The people live with their goats & pile their straw cots by the side of the road during the day & turn them over & sleep right there at night.

Aden is an important refueling stop for cargo & transport ships in this area. Yesterday morning we were lying on our balcony overlooking the sea when a large Australian Navy

---

19   sic – this was how mom spelled it in the letter

ship pulled in. The city was swarming with the sailors in their white shorts & shirts & stockings, till their leave ended at nightfall.

It was the first time they'd been on land since leaving Plymouth, England.

The native costumes are very colorful - the men wearing plaid cotton shirts & white or bright-hued head bands or turbans. The women for the most part are heavily draped & veiled.

More later from Tel-Aviv. Must get those letters typed - it's 7A.M. now & already the heat is pressing in. Much love to all from Herb & Beth X

---

1 August 2006

I looked up again and felt the familiar pain in my chest as I held back the tears. I felt almost angry, as the urgency to explain who she was, to find whom she was, to have her next to me again, in some way burst through.

"Mom grew up in a very protected environment – and was extremely prejudiced in many ways. She did love her creature comforts! I can just picture her in her long full skirts observing the native way of life! "

I smiled at the memory I had in my head of mom standing with her long pleated 1950's skirt billowing around her.

"I would imagine that being a doctor's daughter she also had a different perspective on cleanliness and disease. I do remember grandpa always making us wash our hands when we visited. It was the first thing we did. He had such nice rose water and glycerin liquid soap that he made himself. I can still smell that scent!"

My mind wandered back to that hallway at 159 Cottage St. I could feel the presence of mom and Deb standing there with me as we paused in our walk to the kitchen. I could smell the mustiness of the old house, see the sink with the glass bottles perched on it and smell the sweet scent of the hand lotion and feel again the guilty pleasure we all took as we snuck small bits to rub onto our hands, knowing that grandpa would be angry if we took too much. I pulled myself out of the memory surprised that my hands were so dry and not moist from the lotion. I deflected my mind away from there and started talking again.

"I was reading in Tom Segev's book[20] again and he quotes a memorandum that Dr. Yosef Meir, the general director of the Ministry of Health, wrote about the immigrants at the transit camp in Aden:"

––––––––––

20 *1949: The First Israelis,* by Tom Segev

'...Fifteen luggage buses arrived, packed with 313 nude or half-naked individuals-whether on account of the heat, or from habit, or from lack of clothes. Crowded, filthy, full of sores, their faces stare blankly, silently.' [21]

"There's also a note in the book that: 'Photographs taken inside the planes on the eight-hour, world-to-world voyage, show the immigrants looking frozen with horror.'"

I could hear my mom telling me about the passengers coming on board with their sheep and chickens and felt sad that I had not asked her more questions. I scanned the letter quickly, commenting on sentences I spied.

"Mom did mention that they threw up. Most of them had never flown before. I just can't see her as the stewardess in all of this!"

"Amazing that she loved to co-pilot! Again – who is this woman????"

"She did so love to sunbathe and go to the beach. I remember her dragging us as kids. "

"She wrote well...and spelled pretty well! It's always surprising when I find a word misspelled. Those were the days without spell-check! She was a very smart and well-educated woman."

I could no longer hold back the tide of emotions that were engulfing me. Tears were spilling out of my eyes. I faced where I

---

21 Ministry of Health, internal memorandum-not for publication-following a visit to Aden, September 1949, State Archives, Foreign Ministry, 2397/15

really was and words spilled out with the tears, releasing that knot of pain in my chest.

"August 9th is her birthday..."

"Where is that Kleenex box now? Oh, thank you..."

"Last year she was so proudly walking around in her little pink sneakers that I had bought her."

"We had sandwiches out under the tree. I had bought her cake at Shaws since I hadn't had time to get her the cake from Alden Merrill. She was so disappointed that I hadn't gotten her carrot cake. I wish I had..."

"I had figured she wasn't eating anything I got her so why bother..."

"I need more Kleenex...this box is empty..."

"Thank you..."

"There's so much guilt...you don't get any do-overs either...and it's about little stuff like the cake...or like feeling angry that I had to pay for a cell phone for her...or for a car...bottom line is that is little stuff – a human life is worth so much..."

"Ah well...yes I'll see you next week..."

I stood up and looked around for a moment, getting my bearings. I realized that there was sunshine spilling in through the window. I had survived my walk back through time, and although August would be painful, I was facing it squarely and would pull through it.

2 August 2006 – 6am

For over a year
sleep eluded me.
I tossed restlessly
waiting...waiting for the call.

And, when it came
I was asleep.
Guiltily now
I sleep soundly.

Life on hold
grinding glass
making things
all I could do,
waiting for the end

Now sleep envelops me
warmly like a hug.
Relaxing into it
I awake with a start
wondering...
Will I return?

15 May 1949

Albergo - C.I.A.A.O. - Hotel

Sunday Morning

~~*Saturday*~~

May 15ᵗʰ

ASMARA

(ERITRIA)

Dir. COMM. L. GIANFILIPPI

Telefon i: 21 - 94 - 32 - 31

Telegra : CIAAO - Asmara

Dear Folks,

I had a lot of letters written in Tel-Aviv to bring down & mail on this trip but forgot them in our rush of leaving at 6 A.M. yesterday. I'd written Frances Congdon, Mary-Lou, Aunt Alice Macy,

Bill & Silvia as well as to you. They'll have to go with the other crew on the next trip here - I think there'll be one more.

We ran into several rainstorms above Asmara & circled the field awhile before landing, as the weather wasn't too good. The rainy season finally broke three days ago here & the coolness is heavenly, after Tel Aviv's heat. The food tastes like ambrosia, & particularly so to me since I was hit with Tel-Aviv dysentery on the 11th & haven't had much but tea & soup since till reaching here. The comfort & quiet is wonderful, too. I wish we could have a few days in Asmara to build up to combat Tel-Aviv again! But we'll be leaving on the 20th for the States, if plans go as scheduled. The 54 came into Lydda from Hong Kong just before we left yesterday. Mrs. Maguire is going back to join her husband. He's shuttling between Shanghae & Hong Kong.

We're leaving for Aden, to pick up passengers, at 8 this morning. If we can't get out of Aden before noontime, we'll stay overnight. I want to pick up a few souveniers to bring home from Aden, as that's the best place around here to get native things.

We had coffee at the Cutbush's house when we landed here, & it was good to see them again. Mrs Struppi came to the hotel to say hello & Pattie Gilmore dropped around also, so it was like old home week. I've promised to write them all from the States.

Our route home will be Rome or Paris, Amsterdam, Scotland, Iceland, Newfoundland, Montreal, New York. The planes usually proceed right on to Everett, but Herb will probably be able to arrange it so we can have at least a *day to come to New Bedford & see you & pick up some sheets of mine, etc. <u>We're looking forward to settling in Everett.</u>*

There has been no word from the Macy's since they knew of our marriage. We both enjoy your letters, they mean a lot overseas, & thanks for writing so often. (would like to have been able to peek in on Bill's graduation on the 17ᵗʰ) X

Love to all from

Herb & Beth

---

3 Aug 2006

I walked back into my therapist's office and sat quietly for a while composing my thoughts. She sat in comforting silence with me. The clock on the desk ticked quietly, marking away the minutes. I struggled to put my thoughts in some sort of coherent order. I took a deep breath and began.

"You know it's strange to think that all these letters were written around this time of year – from the time of her death to the time of her birthday…rather a strange coincidence shall we say?"

I watched my therapist's face, looking for support, for guidance, for answers.

"She sounds rather shallow at times... I know she wasn't a great humanitarian... sounds like it was just Herb's job as far as she was concerned and she was there to support him and the crew....I keep trying to want to make her sound like a heroine. But that wasn't who she was. History is just made of normal people..."

I looked at the floor trying to figure out where I was going with this train of thought, forging on, letting it spill out from my mind, through my lips, to the floor.

"I still just keep thinking how strange it must have been to her. To be married overseas; to be on your honeymoon and ferrying Yeminite refuges over to Israel over Arab territory; to have all these people she never met before tromping in and out of her hotel room; to be getting to know the man she married through all of this; to be experiencing different foods; to be alone and sick while waiting for Dad to come back from a trip; to be learning the airline operations and be a key support person for it – It all seems overwhelming. And that my mother, the woman who couldn't drive to Boston without yanking us kids out of school to co-pilot for her, could co-pilot a plane!"

I realized that I was searching for the end of the tumult in side of me. For a way to resolve what was the relationship between my mother and myself: to somehow be forgiven and forgive. I felt frustrated because it seemed like I was going over old ground and couldn't move past it and move on. I wanted relief: Relief from guilt, relief from anger, relief from sadness, ...I shifted forward on the couch, speaking earnestly to my therapist, reaching inside for feelings hoping to let them be free for once and for all.

"It's wonderful and bewildering to see this side of her. Wonderful because it validates the part of me that saw a capable and strong woman as my mother when I was growing up. Bewildering, because of the memories of the latter years of her life, when she had panic attacks taking the bus up to visit me in Boston."

I felt like I was a steam engine that was climbing up hill and running out of steam before I could reach the top. I remembered the "Little Engine that Could" story that my mom used to read to me. It was one of my favorites.

"And wonderful because each letter gives me a connection to her that I don't want to lose. I get almost panicked when I think I might not find any more of them. I want an unending supply to keep me in touch with her the rest of my life!"

The tears welled up again. Oh I was so sick of crying and blowing my nose. I looked around desperately for Kleenex to catch the tears and not disgrace myself by having my nose run down my chin. My therapist handed me a box of Kleenex.

"You've moved the Kleenex box again."

I was feeling almost angry at that change in my environment. I struggled to get into a different space with my emotions. Deflection again.

"I figured out that she must have at some time gone through the letters and been typing them up! I ran across typewritten pages that were the same as letters I later found! She wanted them typed up and saved!"

I smiled for the first time that hour.

"Yes, that makes me feel good that I'm typing them up!"

I threw myself further into my race away from the tears and emotions and into show and tell, a sure-fire way to distract me, knowing that my therapist saw through it all. I reached into my bag and drew out an airmail envelope.

"Look! I found, with the other letters, this old money in an envelope!"

"I remember she had a collection of old coins from her trip too. I used to love playing with them. I wonder what happened to them?"

I placed a letter on the couch next to the money.

18 May 1949

May 18ᵗʰ

Tel-Aviv

Dear Folks,

I wouldn't have mentioned the possibility of our coming home so soon if it hadn't been such a <u>sure</u> thing. Now arrangements have been made for two more Asmara trips & two out of Djibouti, the first trip scheduled for May 1ˢᵗ. After that the plane has to go to Amsterdam for complete overhauling. There are enough Yemenites waiting for entrance here to keep us busy for perhaps 3-6 months more, & it looks as if they're going to be allowed to start moving them into Tel-Aviv right off. Herb has wired N.Y. to ask if we shall accept the contract to move them or bring the plane home. Since there's more money for the company in working the 46 here, it seems pretty certain we'll be staying.

If we do stay, Herb & I are moving to more comfortable living quarters & away from this noisy hotel. Blackie & Ford will be giving up an apartment they have in a house on the waterfront. It will cost us less than living here & be a darn sight better.

We're happy over here together, but I'm awfully sorry I wrote you we'd be home this month. I'll keep taking pictures with my new camera & send them to you as a record of our *doings - am having two rolls developed today that I took in Aden.*

The letter from the Jr.C.C. was waiting when we got back last night. If you see any of the girls - tell them we enjoyed it & it was a lovely, thoughtful thing for them to do. Also two letters from mother - keep writing them please, we love to get them.

Loads of love from us both,

Herb & Beth

---

3 Aug 2006

"I found more pictures:"

And then I placed a collection of pictures next to the letter. I was in full show and tell mode. My therapist picked up one of the pictures.

"This one has a caption on it: 'Tommie Hawk, Herb, Buckie Bradshaw, Ted Stern, Freddie Perino – or the crew trying to stop Blackie from chasing a blonde!'"

"These others look like the wedding in Asmara Eritrea. There are captions on the back of two of the pictures. The guy with the beard signing is the mayor and in the background is Blackie Bradshaw, Dad's co-pilot, and Inspector Cutbrush, in uniform, who is signing in another picture."

3 Aug 2006

Show and tell had worked. I felt happy seeing my father, my support. I prattled on.

"It strikes me so, that someone, who was so close to her parents, would be married without them by her side. Just seems like she must have felt very alone at times."

"I also wonder if they had to do something more once back in the States to make it legal? They got divorced so I assume it was legal! Sure wish I could find that marriage certificate."

My therapist interrupted me, reminding me to breathe and check in with myself. I was angry at being brought back to earth.

"What? I don't want to think about how I feel anymore. She's dead. There's nothing I can do to change that."

"OK – see you next week."

I walked out of the door without looking back.

---

15 July 1949

July 15 - I think

Friday

Dear Folks,

I saw Herb off at 10:30 this morning - to Asmara, Aden & back Sunday night. It sure is lonesome without him! I'm staying home this trip to break up a cold I caught on the way back from the change in temperature from ground to flight. Then too the present batch of refugees they're bringing in are pretty well riddled with syphilis, so I'll wait till they can curtain off a section up front for me again.

Last night we looked at that apartment I told you about. It's not as attractive as where we are now, but has a nice big bathroom & small cupboard for kitchenette, & that is something. There's not even a place here where I can do & hang laundry. Herb is going to look for a two-plate electric cooker & small ice chest in Aden & he's also bringing back meat & eggs. We've made the acquaintance of a former Shanghai man in customs who'll let us bring pretty much anything through duty-free, since he's been used to civilized living, too! The rest we'll smuggle, & I think that's the only way we'll be able to get meat in. There are now only three days a week when they are allowed to serve what meat there is here. There's plenty of fish, but this is a nation of the rottenest cooks imaginable, & they just drop all food into a frying pan filled with rancid grease for a couple of seconds, call it done & serve it swimming in a pool of the grease. The Italians (in Asmara), Chinese, Burmese & Indians all really put thought & serve you a meal it's a work of art & something they can be proud of. Those Chinese can take a few bean sprouts, rice & condiments & turn out one of the best dishes you've ever tasted! The Jews lack imagination & artistry in their architecture, too & the stark atrocities they've turned out for buildings here in Tel-Aviv aren't due entirely to lack of material. They seem to thrive on loud noise & confusion & can't get anything done quietly. I noticed that even during the busiest hours, when there was a crowd waiting to take the ferry from Kowloon to Hong Kong, there was never any pushing or shouting, Chinese, Americans & Englishmen all quietly waited their turn. How different here! Now I'll have to mail this from Asmara - one look at this & the censor here would have apoplexy!

Herb is getting a big steak cooked for me in Asmara, keeping it on the ice box we bought for the plane in Hong Kong during flight, and meeting me with it Sunday night. You get an awful hollow feeling here, so that you're constantly hungry, & when you get that way there's not much but food you can think of! So now I'll put my hair up in oil & go to bed & dream of that steak on Sunday! The breakfast we get here consists of pickled & oiled canned herring, cucumbers, Jewish rye bread (otherwise known as black sawdust), egg flopped in grease, & coffee(?) - at least it goes by that name. Just wait till we have the kitchenette & I can make a breakfast of fluffy scrambled eggs & hot biscuits! (We're going to get a hotplate with small oven & muffin & gingerbread mixes from Aden) The Jews here are all very fat but that's because there's plenty of potatoes & sugar obtainable. We're also flying butter in from Aden or Asmara, & I got loads of Nescafe & evaporated milk, soup & canned fruit & juices in Hong Kong which are stored now with the ships supplies at the airport. Every time we go out we bring a few cans back with us. Brother - are we going to start living in a few days!! We're moving to the new apartment on Thursday. There's just two small white iron cots & one round table, & that makes it rent as a furnished apartment. But it's going to be home, & I'm looking forward to it.

Now to bed - loads of love to all,

X Tinky X

P.S. The 54 crew are all looking forward to going Stateside in a few days. We will probably be here until November - say it quickly! It could be much worse & the main thing is we're together that's what counts!

P.S. I don't know what I'd have done without our vitamins. I wrote from Hong Kong asking if you would please send us some more, plus feosol & proloid to S.T.A.I.R. (our agents) Asmara, Eritrea. The censors here would probably grab them for their own use or sale!

XXX

Herb has shed 17 lbs. since he came to Tel Aviv & I wouldn't say I'm fat! But I'm hoping that when I've had a chance to cook I can put a little weight on us both.

X

We've got a nice letter from Jimmy the other day - the first acknowledgment any of Herb's family have made of our marriage. So I wrote back to him & straightened out a few of the lies Lena has been trying to stuff him with. However, I can't bring myself to write Herb's parents again until there's more civil word from them. There have been a couple of letters from his father to the tune of he hopes Herb likes the bed he has made for himself, & that is all)

---

8 August 2006

I walked into my therapist's office. The fact, that it was the day before mom's birthday, echoed in my head, almost blocking out any other thought. I refused to face it and immediately sat down and went back into show and tell mode, picking up from last week. I read a bit from mom's letter.

"Fascinating! Kit always said that Dad's family rejected the current wife and embraced the past one and they certainly did that with mom!"

"I was reading in one of the history books I bought on Amazon[22] that there was a lot of concern in Israel over the quality of the immigrants they were bringing in, since the main goal of immigration was to increase the defense capabilities of the nation. So they wanted to screen out the undesirables (although they never did). The American JOINT Distribution committee took responsibility for the immigrants who were considered 'unfit'. In at least one group of immigrants the Jewish Agency's representative in Aden reported a large number with venereal diseases. "

And there was concern over the lack of hygiene among the refugees. So I imagine that mom's fears had some basis to them. I feel badly that my first reaction is always to judge her poorly, rather than look for what might be behind her reactions. I'm seeing a person I haven't seen for so many years. And one I never really knew."

I paused as my mind played traitor on me and brought me back to 85 Armour St. My therapist saw the change in my face and asked me what I was thinking.

"I got a flash of mom in the kitchen cooking liver and onions and bacon. It was great! I still like liver and onions to this day! And bacon, well that is a special treat!"

I remembered the game that Deb and I played to see who could be the one eating the last piece of bacon. We would chew each piece slowly, savoring each small bite, trying to fake the other out by taking the longest and then chewing the last piece slowly in front of the other. I trumped her one day by coming to the table early and

---

22 *1949: The First Israelis* by Tom Segev

hiding two pieces of bacon under my plate. She was suspicious but when I sat there with my empty plate she slowly chewed each piece left on her plate, smiling and making satisfied noises and smacking her lips. When she was done I pulled out a piece of bacon from under my plate and, looking right into her eyes, nibbled it, rolling each bite around in my mouth and smiling. She was ready to hit me at the end. And after I finished my second piece in front of her, she did! I pulled myself back to thinking of mom. I thought a moment and realized that my mother really didn't like to cook.

"But she stopped cooking at some point at Suffolk Ave. I wonder what triggered that. She claimed it was the cost of the electric stove but she didn't pay the electric bill – it was subsidized and she's put a tiny amount on it each month but she knew they wouldn't shut it off…"

I remembered the stove with tin covers on the burners and the electricity shut off from them to keep the cats from burning themselves. I could picture the clutter and the derelict condition the kitchen was in. A twinge passed over my face. My therapist followed up immediately by asking if I felt guilty. Feelings poured out of me in the form of words spilling over each other almost too fast to keep up with the thoughts with the speech.

"Yes, I do feel guilty. I think, 'why didn't I do more?', but I also resented having to buy that shit-box of a house so she'd have a roof over her head!"

"I do remember she loved Chinese food – I took her out for it a couple of times when I was trying to get her to eat more. And she ate a fair amount. Took the rest home to eat later even…"

"I can't reconcile in my head this food bit. Deb says mom was anorexic. I think she may have been bulimic too. She was always throwing up when we were young. But she claimed she loved food."

"The amazing part about the letters is that they are bringing some pieces together for me – they are really a gift. I had such trouble in recent years reconciling the woman who I saw with the strong mother that I dimly remembered but internalized. But here in the letters is a woman who enjoyed co-piloting a plane!"

"I was so angry at her for so many years. I think partly because I knew she was in there or at least had been and couldn't understand why my mother was shutting off that capable side of herself. Why she had given up."

"I don't know what else to say. Is it possible for someone to do that to themselves?"

The pain inside was back. I reached inside my bag for another letter, hoping to put salve on the wound.

Undated – 1949

We still have our daughter with us - it does take away some of your privacy but can't be helped, as there's no other available room yet.

We're having our teak wood desk and chest shipped to you to keep for us until we've a home for them in Everett. Please uncrate them and stick them around where you choose. Since they're coming by boat. It may be six weeks before they arrive. We'd be interested in knowing the condition they arrive in, since the shop where we bought them will take care of any damage from transportation. We'd like eventually to order a teak wood dining-room set from the same factory, but are going to wait first and see how the desk and chest stand up in the change of climate. Maguire has bought some before and says it's apt to crack and give at the seams. Ours is well made with interlocking joinings instead of nails, so we're hoping it will stand up better than most. We have the address of the factory, and when we're settled in Everett and know the size and shape of the furniture *we want, we have only to send measurements and descriptions and have sets made up here. I've never liked any furniture so well and do hope it proves practical.*

I'm using my new Parker 51 - Herb got me a blue pen and pencil set here. Everything is cheaper than the States. You can get beautiful watches - Blackie got himself a solid gold Swiss one for $190 that would be at least $250-$300 in the States, and Herb is going to get a Universal Geneva before we leave. Then we'd better all beat it back to Tel-Aviv before we're dead broke!

---

8 August 2006

I sat silent for a while, feeling disappointed, and then said: "I think she may have typed and then rewritten some letters – this one goes on but it's a repeat of others I've found."

I searched around the caverns in my mind avoiding the big hole labeled 9 August and tried to tie something else to that nagging feeling of sadness inside.

"I do wish she had kept some of that furniture…"

My therapist asked me what the date was.

"Oh yes, tomorrow is her birthday."

At that point the sadness, now detected and hooked to the right source, grew and burst forth.

"You've moved the Kleenex box again."

I cried silently for a while, struggling to put it back, the hurt too familiar and tiring. I pulled out another letter from my backpack.

"Do I have time for another letter?"

---

9 July 1949

July 9th

Friday Night

Dear Folks,

It seems strange to see the plane off this evening & not be going along. They left Lydda at 6:15 for a guide run to Aden & will be back tomorrow about 6 or 7 at night. I'm staying here this trip &

getting things organized for our departure for Hong Kong on Monday. Am also getting Alaska Airlines accounts for this operation in shape as well as our own finances, for which I've bought two account books and a filing notebook or portfolio. As well as business manager & secretary, I'm stewardess & nursemaid - having merthiolated & bandaged Blackie's cut fingers before he left & sent the boys off with oranges, cheese & egg sandwiches & orange juice aboard the plane for the trip tonight. I sometimes feel like a mother to them all. Though of course Herb's my biggest baby & a very precious handful & full-time job, which I, of course, enjoy very much.

Last night we had dinner in our room, & then saw a French film - dramatic but good. Today we left for Haifa around 10 A.M. to see about shots & visas. I have all I need for Hong

Kong. Herb has to get Cholera, which he'll do in Aden this trip. Haifa is a lovely town, with beautiful drive from Tel-Aviv, so we had a nice day. Got back here around 4 P.M. & had coffee in our room with Blackie. Now I'm going to put my hair up & take a book to bed, & have the accounts for tomorrow.

The weather's been heavenly here lately, & the Mediterranean is blue & sparkling - a lovely climate.

Lots of love to all,

Tinky XX

We're both _fine_ - everyone says Herb looks years younger since he was married - & I've had no more gallbladder, or whatever it was, trouble.

XX

8 August 2006

The letter sat unread on my lap while my mind wandered through the last 18 months, visions of mom flashing through on fast-forward.

"I remember her acting like Deb's baby when she was very ill this past year."

My therapist pointed out the time and mentioned it was time to wrap up.

"Our time is up?"

I didn't want to leave. I felt almost frantic. There was so much left to say. My therapist pointed out the obvious.

"Yes I know I didn't talk about tomorrow."

I sat very still and looked down at my hands folded over the letter. Inside I was screaming so loudly I was almost numb and feared moving in case it should spill out. Anger and frustration pounded at the inside of my chest. I had frittered away so much time. My therapist mentioned writing down how I was feeling.

"I will do some writing. I did do some painting last week. Here it is:"

I handed my therapist a printed copy of my painting that I had scanned in the night before. My therapist respectfully took the image, holding it lightly in her hands and asked if I wanted to talk about it.

"No, I don't feel like talking about it yet."

But I kept on talking. The words spilling out quickly, unbidden and unrestrained.

"Yes I do feel angry...depressed too. But as I painted this it became less black than it was in the beginning. I guess that's a good thing, hey?"

"She loved animals. Especially birds. 'Hearing the birds sing' was her expression for being happy. "

"Why BRP? I feel like she died twice. Part of who she was died along the way. I relate that to Beth Richardson Perry, her maiden name. She died in the end as Beth Richardson Macy. She always kept his name. But I'm reading about a 1949 woman who I didn't see at the end. And as I'm burying her, I'm sad and angry."

"I really don't want to talk about it..."

"It makes me sad and angry and I don't know what to do."

"See you next week. Oh that's right, I forgot. You're on vacation next week. OK..."

I sat there feeling a wave dragging me down, a weightiness in my shoulders, feeling them sag, the pounding in my head begin again, my feet unable to make their way towards the door.

"Thursday? That's right. It's only Tuesday. Sure. I can do Thursday this week. Thanks."

The room seemed to lighten at the thought that I would soon have a second chance to work out what I was feeling about tomorrow. I stood up and walked out the door feeling lightheaded and determined to do my writing.

---

8 August 2006

Anger

Boiling inside

Umbilical cord broken

In place far too long

Generations tied to each other

Finally set free

---

9 August 2007

Mom's rose bush was happily blossoming small red flowers and sprouting new leaves. A bird's white feather lay near it. I placed the feather gently next to a seashell in her garden and plucked out some stray pieces of grass. Tears quietly streamed down my face. I went inside the house to write down my feelings.

9 August 2006 – 8:06am

Happy Birthday mom
It's a beautiful day outside.
You always said
your birthday had beautiful weather.
I hope you're up there
eating everything you want.
And everything you deprived yourself of.
Eat full fat ice cream!

I imagine you up there with Allie today.
I can see the two of you in my mind.
You look about 35 or 40.
Allie's in her 50's.
I wonder what ages you look like to you?
Do people up there morph to any age they want?

I need to move on mom…
I'm sick of holding all this guilt.
It's time I let go.
And time to really
embrace and live my life.
I've spent too many years unconscious.

I gave you the gift of my love.
And I continue to give that to you.
They say "you can't take it with you."
Well, I think they're wrong –
Some things you can.

Happy Birthday mom
Is it still your birthday if you're gone?
What should we do with this day?
A day of memories...
Of joy? Or of mourning?

Last year you were here.
Today you're gone
Life is so fleeting
We just never know
when that last day will be
So embrace life for all that it is
Be happy

So Happy Birthday, mom
I will find a way each year
to mark this day
As one of love and celebration
It's a beautiful day, just as you said.
Why then am I crying?

3 June 1949

June 3rd

5:30 A.M. on the C46 enroute Asmara

Dear Folks,

What hours we keep - but we do have fun!

Herb spent most of yesterday chasing around the American & British Consul offices in Tel-Aviv to get landing rights for the trip to Hong Kong. We had dinner sent up to our room at the hotel at 10 P.M. - had schnitzel, breaded veal - got some sleep for a couple of hours & left the hotel at 1 A.M. They must have been having some sort of trouble at the airport, for there were armed guards around & boxer watchdogs to escort us out onto the field to the plane. Of course it was pitch dark, & the coyotes were baying, the watchdogs kept stiffening up, & they even brought one of the dogs on board the plane & had him sniff around - real eerie! Redlinger, Ted & Herb have this light & they fixed a place for me in the cockpit so I wouldn't have to sit alone in the main part of the plane.

There's just about room for the radio operator & pilot's seats up front, but we propped a couple of pillows & spread some blankets on the floor & wedged me in behind the pilots' chairs - real comfortable, for I fell fast asleep.

The sun's just come up - I'm sitting back in the plane now, & Herb's crawled on top of the big gas tank in here to catch some sleep while Redlinger takes over. We hadn't planned to make such an *early morning trip to Asmara. We've just the one radio operator now, & Ted's had three hours sleep the past two nights. But we're rushing some Streptomycin that's needed to save a life in Aden. Since we've no more business there, & B.O.A.C. has a plane from Asmara to Aden at 9 A.M., & we do have a load ready in Asmara - off we went.*

We'll be staying in Asmara until Sunday night or Monday - a nice long time. I think there's a possibility of one more Asmara trip, & then we're pulling out of here before they nab us for any long-term contracts.

Lots of love to all,

Tinky X

---

10 Aug 2006

I walked into my therapist's office. It seemed smaller than it had on Tuesday. I leaned forward in my seat on the couch and started talking immediately, gesturing quickly with my hands, looking directly at my therapist, letting the long overdue feelings spill from my lips. She also leaned forward in her wicker chair, letting me roll on, occasionally interjecting questions.

"Yesterday was so hard. I couldn't stop crying. It was so hard to get through work. I kept pretending I had allergies. It surprised me - I don't cry every day any more. It's more like a constant dull ache now."

"What? Yes I do think I sometimes avoid feeling or thinking about her. It just hurts when I do. And there's nothing I can do about it. She's gone."

"I need the wastebasket..."

"I was talking to my step-mom about the research I was doing. She says there was a lot of controversy after Israel was founded about whether or not to support Israel, even within the American Jewish population. There were so many emotions wrapped around what was going on in that area in 1949: U.S. fear of Soviet dominance, greed for oil reserves, Jewish longing for a safe haven after the atrocities of the war, Arabs angry at having their homes and property taken from them when Israel was formed, yet in it all there's people just living their lives and doing their jobs. That's what is to me so interesting about the letters. It is the every day mundaneness of it all that comes through. 'Yesterday I was walking the streets of New Bedford and today I'm flying from Aden to Tel-Aviv...and oh yes, I hope they let me co-pilot.' Meanwhile refuges, who may never have seen a plane before, are terrified and crammed into the back of the plane with their livestock, having babies, trying to light fires, causing fear in the crew. And Dad who always said 'he just took a plane from point A to point B', was flying over hostile territory with a dubious amount of fuel in the tanks. And mom sits there behind Dad, writing notes home to the 'Folks'. I wish I knew what was really going through her mind. I wonder if it all really terrified her and that's why she never flew anywhere again?"

"We never connected as adults – never could get over the rift that happened between the mother and daughter."

"I never got past wanting her to be my mother…"

"It was wonderful when she was there…"

"This could have been such a great bonding experience to talk about as I started traveling the world. But we spent so many years angry at each other. First me angry at her during my high school years and then her angry at me for changing custody. And then a brief truce in the middle and then resentment at supporting her and finally anger again on both sides over things I've hashed over enough…"

"I want the clock turned back! I want to discover these 5 years ago…to have had a last few years of healing with her."

"She asked the Angel of Death (who she claimed visited her last August) for a final year and then she did nothing with that year!"

"There are so many emotions here – confusion, want, anger, hurt, sadness…"

I finally paused and looked around the room. Daylight was streaming in through the window over my therapist's right shoulder, dappling patterns on the oriental rug. A squirrel was playing in the tree outside the other window, while a small bird darted to and fro the feeder. Life abounded outside and I was trapped in the world of my head, a past that I needed to get through and move on from, struggling to understand mom's world so I could let her go, let the past go, live in today without this thing that lived inside of me every day – this blackness, this sadness, this anger. And above all I just wanted my mother back. But I didn't know whom that person was that I wanted back. What had I made her to be and who was she really?

I took a deep breath and then bent down and searched in my backpack for a letter.

---

3 May 1949

May 3ʳᵈ Tuesday A.M.

Dear Mum & Dad,

I'll let Herb mail this from Aden or Asmara on his next flight there. It'll reach you quicker & escape the censorship here. I'm sorry not to have written more often, but we've been busy getting settled at the Yarden. We have a lovely room there & it seems quite like home.

Yesterday we bought a "wandering jew" - most appropriate - plant in a little wall bracket for decoration, some plates, knives, forks, & spoons, & then had a great time picking out food for our first meal at home. We had tomato soup with rice, salmon, applesauce, spaghetti with tomato sauce, crackers & honey & coffee. Later we went to see "The Best Years of Our Lives" - then came back & had some bullion with Ted Stern in our room.

Yesterday they went on daylight saving time here. It's 10:30 now. I've just made some Nescafe' for I just woke up. Isn't that awful! But we were up late last night. These days we have when Herb isn't flying & we're together are wonderful! The times he's gone I have plenty to do catching up with the laundry. I ironed three shirts yesterday morning & was quite proud of the results! It takes a long time to do cotton goods because the electric current is low & the iron never gets really hot enough.

I just tried to wake Herb up to give him his coffee but he just grunted, so I drank it myself! We're very happy here & both well.

Ted Stern took the enclosed pictures in the diningroom of the Crescent Hotel, Aden. They're not too good. I'm going to see if we can borrow a camera & take some more to send to you. Mail from home must be going to Asmara. Herb will pick any up on his next trip there, but Alaska is flying more to Aden now rarely does go to Asmara.

Bob Maguire has gone with the 54th to Shanghai - probably be gone about a week. Then the 54 will most likely go Stateside. No further news on plans for the 46, but it is still scheduled to return home May 20th unless they can obtain a waiver for it's stay here. We were originally due to proceed to Rome or Germany to fly the "Lift" but a big cut down on that deal has put a lot of pilots out of work. By accepting the position he was offered & staying over here, Herb probably saved his job with the company.

Loads of love to all,

Herb & Beth XX

Just found this letter, written sometime ago, but will send it along now.

X

May 5th

10 Aug 2006

I handed the letter to my therapist with a picture I had found. The letter was written in mom's neat handwriting on crinkly thin airmail paper and the picture was yellowed with age, both relics of another age. The years in between hung around them and in me.

"I would love to find out more information about the refugees and the "Lift". I just bought this book *1949: The First Israelis* by Tom Segev. It seems packed with information. It talks about the Austerity program that mom mentions in her letters. Apparently it cost $2,000 - $3,000 to absorb each immigrant so the Israeli deficit was running over 200 million dollars. They received around $100M from Jewish communities in the United States but had to take out loans. And then they had a huge chunk of the budget going to defense. So they started an austerity program, 'which included strict price controls, rationing of food and services, raw materials and foreign currency. The program was designed to ensure a minimum standard of living for the entire population, locals and newcomers alike...The People were not hungry, but they had to make do with frozen codfish and dehydrated eggs, obtained in exchange for coupons after standing in line for hours.'[23] So of course all this kicked off a black market in food and other goods. No wonder they had to bribe customs to get things in!"

"Dad and mom are really skinny in the pictures of them over there. No wonder food was on her mind all the time!"

---

23 *1949: The First Israelis* by Tom Segev

"They look happy though, don't they? Well, at least mom does!"

10 Aug 2006

I peered closely at the picture, mentally cursing the bifocals that were no true replacement for the eyesight I had when I was younger. I looked for me in both of my parents in that picture while I continued talking about the era they came from.

"According to Mr. Segev's book, they had coupon books that the government distributed, first to retailers like grocers, greengrocers and butchers and later even to the restaurants. And the coupons sold to the public were to try and 'maintain a minimum daily ration of calories, approximately 2,600 per day.'[24]

"Mom said Tel-Aviv was expensive but Mr. Segev states 'Prices were low, but, ... , The daily burden of it fell primarily on the women, who spent much of their time standing in line...lines for eggs and milk, meat and fish. It often took as long as two hours, and sometimes it was all in vain – by the time the housewife's turn came the rations had run out and she had to go home empty-handed.' I cannot envision my mother or even the woman writing these letters doing that! She's having a hard time trying to do laundry without a washing machine!"

"Time's up already? OK."

"See you in two weeks..."

---

14 Aug 2006

Hands
Tell so much
Mom's ring
Foreign on Deb's hand
Deb's fingers
Long and slender
Older than remembered
Nervously twisting

24　*1949: The First Israelis* by Tom Segev

Hands
A reflection of the inner self
Mom's hands
In the end gnarled and misshapen
Clutching, afraid
So much lost
In days gone by
Strong hands

Hands
Able to fix anything
To hammer, cook, sew,
paint, drive, light cigarettes.
Capable hands
That could caress,
make dolls, knit,
hit.

Hands
Gesturing our inner thoughts
Mom's hands
Always busy
Creating
Reaching out
Pulling back
Finally still.

18 Aug 2006

Different Worlds
Only 3 years
Separate us
my sister and me
But we are worlds apart
I
paint a picture
of depression and rage
She
sees a picture
of love
burning away cold grief
I paint my world
of happiness trapped
behind grey clouds
and yet she
sees a final resting spot
for mom
I am unable to reply
Unable
to find words
to close that gap
One that always was
but one
that has grown so much
throughout the years.

3 July 1949

July 3, 1949

Sunday

Dear Folks,

It was wonderful to hear you yesterday. The reception was pretty good on this end considering the distance it had to cover. I know it was an ungodly hour to call, but you have to take the calls when you can get them through, and they'll put them through only between 1&3 P.M. Work on the plane being not yet finished, we'll probably leave here Tuesday noon - overnight in Bangkok + the rest of the trip with stops to refuel only.

As if he hadn't had enough trouble already, yesterday Maguire fell down the hotel stairs & sprained his ankle quite badly - tore the ligament. We took him to the hospital for X-ray to make sure it wasn't a break. He stayed in our room last night & had a pretty rocky night.

How much longer we'll be in Tel-Aviv depends on what Maguire has to report when he comes there on the 28th of July from seeing Wooten to make arrangements for suitable living quarters & decent pay for us there. Til then, we'll be back at the Yarden.

We're shipping home two chests - one we got in Aden & one we bought here - a secretary & a coffee table. They'll arrive in Boston - addressed to you - & when you get notice of their arrival (in about 6 weeks) call the Customs House in New Bedford & they'll give you information about getting them to New Bedford. If we can get them on a ship before we leave, they'll arrive in New Bedford with $35.00 to $40.00 due. If that happens to be the case, be sure to let us know how much the charges were so that we can reimburse you. Will you please call in a cabinet-maker to look at the teak wood chest & secretary to see if oiling, waxing, or standing the feet in linseed oil would help prevent the wood from cracking. The change in climate is apt to affect it. We're pretty pleased with our new furniture.

Loads of Love,

X Tinky X

22 Aug 2006

I put the letter down in disgust and looked up at my therapist, sighed and said: "More furniture descriptions..."

I looked around the room, taking in the furniture in this room, wondering how I would describe it, or even if I would. Would I describe the emotions, the people, or just the furniture? Describing furniture seemed to be a way to avoid the rest.

"How do I feel? I don't know...I guess I feel disappointed in some way...almost angry at her..."

I felt anger well up inside of me tightening my muscles in my back and neck. My hands balled into fists.

"I want more! I want more of who she was, what she felt, what was going on around her. It's like she disappeared from the real world and hid in a world of teak furniture!"

I thought of what I said and flashed to a woman who had limited skills with dealing with the world, thrown overseas with a bunch of strangers and a new husband that she didn't know that well either, apart from the family she had been welded to most of her life. The letter made sense.

"... oh... that kinda fits..."

The anger mixed now with sadness while understanding her clashed with being angry at her, angry at my own needs not being met. The furniture in the room seemed blurred.

"My head hurts...I can't do this right now... Maybe there will be something in the next letter I found..."

8 July 1948

Eroute Bankok from Hong Kong, July

8:30 A.M.

Dear Folks,

Well, here we are on the first lap of our return journey to Tel-Aviv. We started takeoff yesterday noon & had a close call when the rt. engine failed. Luckily, it happened before we were airborne, but the plane went careening off the runway & almost rammed some parked planes. The gas tanks had been checked in the morning, but there's such high humidity at Hong Kong that the water of condensation had collected in the gas tank so that the engine was feeding on that instead of the gas. So we went back to the hotel, took the lunches the airport had put up for us, & all had a picnic in Freddie & Dorothy's room to keep Dorothy company. She's suffering from the same thing I had in Tel-Aviv, being newly arrived from the States & her intestines not yet acclimated to the bacteria in foreign food!

This morning we got a 7:30 start, & all went well on takeoff. The airport at Hong Kong is surrounded by steep mountains with just one clear passage out over the sea, & we have a full capacity load - mostly baggage of Jewish refugees Alaska has flown from Shanghai to Lydda. We also have a good big supply of tinned meat, fruit, fruit juices, Nescafe' & evaporated milk for our own use in Tel-Aviv. We'll have to sneak a few through customs at a time - you can't bring a darn thing into Palestine. They want

to force people to use native products. Ah me -
Promised Land here we come!

Herb bought father a beautiful Swiss made,
self-winding, Rolex watch for your birthday
and in appreciation of all you've done for him -
fanny shots, etc. It's a very lovely watch, with
second hand for taking pulses. But we can't send
it to you because of the import duty that would
have to be paid, so we'll have to wait until we
come back ourselves. He also got a lovely little
gold Waltham for mother. We'll wear them into
the States to get them through customs. You see,
in Hong Kong watches are minus the luxury
tax they have in the States, & that knocks off
quite a bit. We're bringing back umbrellas for
the custom men at Bombay, & silk & whiskey for
the Lydda customs. I think it's an awful racket,

but they can make it mighty unpleasant for you if you don't oil their palms, & when we left Lyyda they gave us a list of things they wanted from China. You get them or else, brother, you just never get through customs with all your stuff. Isn't that like a bunch of Jews!

Herb & I had an injection for Bubonic Plague by the hotel doctor the day before yesterday. There's a follow-up shot due in 7 days, & we can get that in Asmara. We fly through Plague areas & this hot weather brings on the epidemics. The shots didn't bother us at all. Great part of the world this is - according to the health maps we're in the greatest section of the world for yellow fever, smallpox, typhoid & plague. Thank heavens for inoculations! What a clean healthy place the good old U.S.A. is, *where you can actually drink water from a tap faucet! Lots of love to all,*

X Tinky X

---

22 Aug 2006

I put the letter down and smiled. The room seemed clearer now. The ache in my head was less.

"That's more like it! She used to tell one story of the engine failing but that was while flying over Arab territory, not on takeoff. There was such an amazing richness of stories she could have told us! Instead, she gives a great picture of the ugly American. There making history and not a clue – worried about her teak furniture arriving home safely. No compassion for the people she's flying around: just revulsion at the dirtiness. No wonder she never wanted to travel again with that attitude. It fits. This is much more like the mother I knew. Dr.'s daughter grows up privileged and tip-toes around, superior, through the rest of the world, only to end up in a run down shack in New Bedford with filth all around her."

Suddenly visions of mom flashed through my head like an old movie on fast forward. Mom looking tired, hair screwed up on top of her head, an apron tied around her waist, eating bread dipped in bacon fat in the kitchen at 85 Armour St.; Mom hanging laundry on the line in the back yard at Armour St. while flies circled the nearby garbage cans; Mom lying on the battered couch at 30

Suffolk Ave, with her Oxygen machine taking up most of the tiny living room; ...I let out a large sigh.

My therapist leaned forward, asking me if I was angry.

"Yes, I am angry."

I touched my forehead and brushed away the visions of mom, and worked to find something positive.

"But she's right – we are lucky to be able to drink tap water, I guess - I actually prefer my way of life with a cistern. Conserving water is something we Americans just can't grasp."

I saw my therapist raise and eyebrow and stopped myself from going off on a water saving tangent and returned to mom.

"It must have been very scary for her, you know? And fear often makes that ugliness of condemning others. I think she had no outlet for that fear too. She couldn't let on to her folks – she was keeping the brave face up in the letters. She couldn't tell Dad. She needed to be part of his adventure and not a drag on it. She must have felt very lonely in all of these feelings. If she even recognized them. She did recognize her loneliness when Dad was gone."

I carefully handed my therapist a New Bedford Standard Time's clipping I had found of mom's engagement announcement. It was yellowed with age and had that faint musty smell of antiquity.

"But think on it. She was a society 'deb' from 1940's New Bedford thrown into the Middle East of 1949. On her honeymoon no less!!! Stuck in hotel rooms with the crew popping in and out all the time or even worse having to share rooms with strangers."

"And a Dr.'s daughter, brought up to respect sanitation and proper treatment of disease, thrown in to very unsanitary conditions with fears of the Bubonic Plague!"

"It's amazing she kept her sanity in all of it!"

I handed my therapist an old yellowed clipping with mom's picture on it and a letter. She looked at them and then looked expectantly back at me.

10 July 1949

July 10th 8:45 A.M.

Enroute Bankok to Calcutta

Dear Folks,

The houseboy at the Frocaders Hotel awoke us this morning at 4:45 - very effectively, by switching on all the lights & bringing tea. We'd gone to bed at 9 o'clock last night, so it wasn't too hard to get up. Our agent had the station wagon ready to take us to the field, and breakfast waiting there. The weather forecast map shows some rough weather ahead from here to Calcutta, & right now we're flying through pretty dense clouds.

Yesterday afternoon I got a birthday present for Herb, since we'll most likely be in Tel-Aviv on the 2ⁿᵈ of October, & you can't buy anything there. They have lovely genuine alligator belts with silver buckles, & I got him one and an etched silver cigarette lighter. I also got two darling dancing dolls in Bangkok dress for Peggy, since I'm starting a foreign doll collection for her while we're overseas to get them. She probably won't enjoy them till she's a good deal older. I get quite a kick out of them myself! Herb got a birthday present for me, too, though of course he wouldn't tell me what! When we get back to Tel-Aviv we're starting on an Austerity program of our own, financially. That's a good place to be on one, because things cost so much you're not tempted to buy. We spent pretty heavily at

Hong Kong, but it's most likely the only time we'll be there. While it may hit hard now, it's a saving for the future since we've got Xmas & birthday presents for almost every-body in advance. A lot of them are being shipped home in the chests - so just peek at them & put them away, because you may be looking at your own Xmas present!

Now to see if the boys want any coffee -

More later & lots of love,

X Tinky X

22 Aug 2006

I took the letter and picture back from my therapist.

"I found this in the letter:"

"She obviously never made that scrapbook."

"I wish I knew how long she was overseas. I wonder if her wedding certificate is in the things that Deb got. I know she had it when we were young. It's all in Arabic. As a child I used to wonder if they had really gotten married."

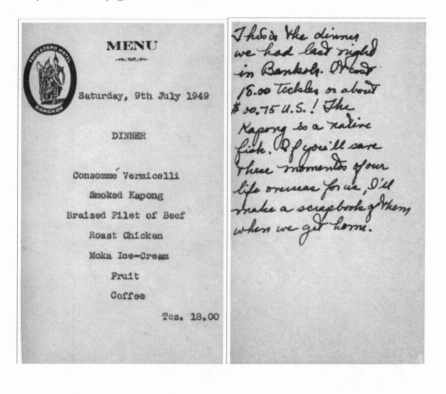

"I found more pictures too! I love the one of Dad filling mom's cigarette lighter from the plane's tank!"

Rickshaw coolie posed in front of hotel.

Enroute Jerusalem from Tel-Aviv

Chas & Ford were bargaining for one of the native smoking pipes.

Front entrance Peninsula Hotel, Kowloon.

Ford in foreground - Cohen lying on engine - & Herb - after fixing the oil leak.

Herb is filling my cigarette lighter from the fusilage tank !

"I feel rather numb. And then it just hits me every once and a while that she's gone. It's like a knife cutting through my chest."

I sat there feeling lost and looked up at my therapist waiting for her to speak.

"OK – I'll see you next week…oh yes, I'd like it if we could do Thurs again. Thanks."

---

30 May 1949

May 30th

Dear Folks,

Just learned the fellows haven't been mailing my letters - they forgot. Now I don't know what news you have & what you haven't. Anyway; you must have my cable that we're going to Hong Kong - in about a week now. Alaska Airlines will have some work for us there - Herb thinks for a couple of months. By then, there'll be some more Yemenites ready to be moved here & we may be back on that, but are hoping for a chance to get home for awhile first.

We got back to Tel-Aviv yesterday from a trip to Jerusalem, & we certainly enjoyed it. Mr. Simon & Mr. Schweide from JOINT went with us, & since they both used to live there, could show us around.

I'm going with Herb on his next trip to Djbouti & to Asmara. The alternate crew have been making the flights to let him run the business end.

No mail from home for over a week - guess it must be because you thought we were on our way home.

Much love to all,

Tinky X

24 Aug 2006

I walked into my therapist's office ready to roll on a show and tell ride. As I sat down on the couch I handed her a letter. She glanced at it and handed it back, waiting for me to speak about it.

"I wasn't sure what JOINT was. I found this on the web:" [25]

I pulled a printout from my backpack and handed it to her.

American Jewish Joint Distribution Committee (JDC) is a United States Jewish charitable organization with the declared mission to "serve the needs of Jews throughout the world, particularly where their lives as Jews are threatened or made more difficult."

Known colloquially as "the Joint," (sometimes capitalized as "JOINT") the organization focuses its effort on non-sectarian disaster relief, rescue of Jews that are in imminent danger, relief from hunger and other hardship, cultural renewal, and transitional assistance for individuals who are displaced or have immigrated. The organization no longer limits itself to the humanitarian needs of Jews and operates a number of initiatives to help all people in need throughout the world, including recent drives to alleviate the situation in the Sudan, Indian Ocean tsunami relief, and the 2005 Kashmir earthquake.

The Joint has three operating principles related to: being non-partisan and non-political, providing empowering assistance, and building strategic alliances with other organizations that take over responsibility for what the Joint helped start.

---

25 http://en.wikipedia.org/wiki/
    American_Jewish_Joint_Distribution_Committee

Founding and World War I

The Joint was founded in 1914 when Henry Morgenthau, Sr., then ambassador to the Ottoman Empire, requested funds from Louis Marshall and Jacob H. Schiff to alleviate famine among Palestinian Jews. As World War I led to violence and persecution of Jews also in Russia and Poland, the Joint undertook a number of initiatives to sustain the Jewish communities there, including the establishment of credit unions, agricultural training, and other relief works.

[edit]

Agro-Joint

The Joint also worked with the Soviet governmental agencies OZET and Komzet to equip and train more than 600,000 Jews to adopt agricultural labor in Ukraine and Crimea as part of the Soviet collectivization program. This effort was discontinued in 1938 when Agro-Joint was expelled from the USSR.

[edit]

World War II

The Joint helped 250,000 German Jews and 125,000 Austrian Jews emigrate between 1933 and 1939 and continued underground relief efforts throughout World War II to Yugoslavia and Poland. It assisted Jewish refugees wherever possible; one such effort was helping thousands of European Jews in Shanghai ghetto to survive the war. The organization moved its European headquarters from Paris to Lisbon and then back to Paris when it was liberated.

[edit]

Post-war years

After the war, the Joint provided relief to over 700,000 Jewish survivors in Europe, many of them in displaced persons camps. Offices were established in Buenos Aires to facilitate immigration to Latin America. When the State of Israel was established in 1948, the Joint set up training and other facilities to ease the transition of immigrants. The organization helped with the immigration of more than 440,000 European Jews to Israel.

The Joint spread its coverage in the following years, making efforts on behalf of Jews in the Soviet Union, Yemen, Iraq, Ethiopia, and elsewhere. A transit center was set up in Ladispoli in Italy for Jewish emigrants from Eastern European countries.

I handed her another printout:
"I also found this info:"[26]

U.S. Assistance to Israel

HISTORY I

* U.S. assistance to Israel began in 1949 with a $100 million Export-Import Bank Loan.

From 1949-65, U.S. aid averaged $63 million per year. 95% was economic development assistance and food aid.

---

26 http://telaviv.usembassy.gov/publish/mission/amb/assistance.html

MILITARY ASSISTANCE I

> * *Military Grants (FMF) - $46.9 Billion from FY1949 to FY2004*
> *U.S. Assistance to Israel: Highlights*

ECONOMIC

> **Economic Grants (ESF) - $29.8 Billion (1949 to 2004)*

EGYPT

> **Total U.S. Assistance, 1948 - 2004: $60 Billion*

"It somehow feels more real to know more about the things that mom mentions in her letters. I want to read another letter. As long as I can read them then she hasn't really left me."

I carefully pulled another letter from the backpack and gently opened it and read bits of it to my therapist.

23 May 1949

May 23rd

YARDEN HOTEL/130, BEN-YEHUDA St.,
TEL-AVIV / PHONE 3732

Dear Folks,

I write as often as there's any news to tell. Things have been very uncertain for the past few days. It looks now as if we'll be leaving for Hong Kong shortly. Will let you know when news is more definite.

Loads & <u>loads</u> of love to all,

Tinky XX

May 23rd

Dear Folks,

This will probably astonish you, & I guess mother can sympathize - seems for two weeks I've been building up to a nice gall bladder attack, & the night before last it hit with a vengeance. Boy, that was no fun - the Tel-Aviv blues were child's play in comparison! Herb called a doctor when it got bad around midnight. He says there's been a series of gall bladder attacks lately due to the greasy cooking hereabouts & faulty refrigeration of fats during Kom Seine. He fixed me up with Depancol - put out by Maltine in N.Y. - Donnatotal, & Dolorex suppositories - containing codeine. He told me to take my vitamins & wrote out a special diet eliminating fats, cold drinks, fried foods, and roughage. I'm to stick to that for 3-4 weeks.

We're rather hoping to be out of this hell-hole by then, but no word from Maguire or New York so far as to what we should do. Ran temp 100.3° yesterday morn., so spent day in bed, but feeling much better today, & guess mother knows how it is when I say it's heavenly to be able to take a deep breath & not feel that pain any more!

The C46 was due back from Aden night before last but there's no word on it, which is queer. Herb has cabled Aden agents to see if they know what's up, in Asmara!

No mail from home for some time & I do miss it. Maybe there'll be one today. Hope all are well.

Yesterday was cool & rainy, but today the sun is out so guess we'll go to the beach when I'm finished washing out some things.

Loads of love to all - will write more from

Asmara,

Tinky X

P.S. - Sent you some pictures from here. Hope you get them. X

---

24 Aug 2006

I rolled on like a car out of control, unable to put the brakes on long enough to stop gliding over the surface facts and pick up the feelings underneath.

"I wonder if that was the precursor of mom's aversion to food with fat in it? I also wonder if that's why she ended up finally dying of cirrhosis of the liver? Perhaps that organ wasn't functioning right from way back? It may have been what caused her to be anorexic. I remember her throwing up a lot when we were growing up. Also she was a great belcher! And her skin was always a darker color – we always thought that was because she sunbathed a lot. Or that there was a piece of family history that no one was admitting to!"

"She also mentioned that her mother would understand – I wonder if Gagi[27] also had problems with her gall bladder. Sure do hope it isn't from something hereditary! - Although I've never had

---

27   Grandma Perry

any problem like this. Again – it sure would have been nice if she had communicated more."

"And then again in another letter I found she dismissed this whole incident as being homesick. It was always so hard to determine what was real when mom was ill."

I thought of mom's food quirks, the huge salad she served for one Thanksgiving dinner, the stove that was rarely used after we left Armour St., and wondered how much had a medical root to it and how much was psychosomatic. I handed to my therapist an article I had printed out as part of my search for the answer to that question.

"Here's what I found on the web about gall bladder:[28]"

Gall Bladder Symptom List

The following is a basic list of gall bladder disease symptoms:

Gall Bladder Symptom 1 - Jaundice

As you may already know, the gall bladder is a holding vessel for bile flowing from the liver to the intestines. The symptoms of disease may vary, but the first and most obvious symptom is jaundice. If the skin becomes jaundiced, then we know that there is most likely an issue with the Gall Bladder or liver. Jaundice can either turn the skin yellow or orange depending on the type. With this, the whites of the eyes often take on a yellow color as well. Jaundice is the result of the liver not properly breaking down old blood and

---

28 http://www.skyeherbals.com/pages/gall2.html

transforming it into bile. This can be the result of either the liver not function-
ing properly, or jaundice can indicate a blockage of the gall bladder.

Gall Bladder Symptom 2 - Gall Bladder Pain Symptoms

Gall Bladder Pain Symptom List - Types of Pain

1. Sporadic pains in the middle of the upper abdomen, or just below the ribs on the right side.

2. The pain may spread to the right shoulder or between the shoulder blades.

3. The pain can be accompanied by nausea and vomiting and some-times excessive wind.

4. The attack can last from a few minutes to two to three hours before getting better.

5. The frequency and severity of attacks is very variable.

6. Attacks can be triggered by eating fatty foods such as chocolate, cheese or pastry.

7. It can be difficult to distinguish the pain from other diseases, such as: gastric ulcer, back problems, heart pains, pneumonia and kidney stones.

Certain symptoms indicate that there is a higher risk of danger and require immediate medical attention. These include:

1. Fever

2. Sweating

3. Chills

4. Jaundice

5. Yellow eyes

6. Yellow skin

7. Persistent pain

8. Clay-colored stools ("Light Colored Stools" or "Pale Stools")

Gall bladder attack symptoms often follow fatty meals, and they may occur during the night. Other gallstone symptoms include

* Abdominal bloating

* Recurring intolerance of fatty foods

* Colic

* Belching.

* Gas

* Indigestion.

---

24 Aug 2006

"Pretty nasty...I'd change my eating habits too if I had that!"

I finally stopped and took a deep breath.

"How do I feel? OK, I guess. I'm not crying much any more. Every once and a while something will hit me but it's like life goes on. Mom always used to say that too."

"Time to go? OK see you next week."

I stood up to leave, paused on my way out the door and looked back at my therapist.

"It just seems like we're not getting anywhere. I should be done by now."

"OK, I'll try and do some writings again."

"Bye."

"Yes, I'll see you Thurs."

25 Aug 2006

I see you in my mind
Alive
Vital
Walking briskly
Laughing
And it strikes me
You are younger than I am now

You said
I will live on in spirit
And you do
You should be happy with that

In my mind
In my heart
Always a part of me
Of my life
Of my thoughts
Never far away
There to touch
If I so dare
If I can bear to do so

For so many years
You were older
And then for a short while

I was the caretaker
And now
You are many ages
And I am left here

I move on
Go through my life
But there is always a feeling
A feeling of something more
And something less

There's a depth to the world now
In an invisible sense
A spiritual sense
If you so believe
I do
I know you are there
Wherever that may be

And I am here
The pain now deeper
And quieter
But always waiting
To be touched

You are here
But you are not really
You are young, vital,
happy, and alive
A shadow in my mind

You live on in spirit
Be happy
I miss you so

They say that you mourn for a year
Perhaps so
But I'll miss you all my life

---

9 July 1949

July 9ᵗʰ

Dear folks,

Here we are back in Bangkok. Herb is having a rest, since he flew all the way over, & I've just got up from mine & had a cup of tea. Now we've reached the beginning of the district where you have to swap from drinking coffee to drinking tea. The coffee in China was delicious, even better than the tea, to me, but from now on thru Tel-Aviv it will be unpalatable. We're going to walk around & take a few pictures & then get to bed early, because we'll have to be up at 4:45 tomorrow morning. We're both fighting a bout with dysentery, no doubt from the Chinese dinners, & if hotel eating in the States is risky, what must it be here! You wrote that we should both put on weight, & I sure wish we could, but it seems that when you do start to look a bit rotund & pleased with yourself, along comes the old dysentery & knocks it right off! Besides which being in a constant bath of perspiration is no help! I think I could wring out Herb's shirt five minutes after he puts it on, & when I sit down & cross my legs I can feel the old perspiration start running off in rivulets, till I'm afraid there'll be a puddle on the floor at my feet. But I'm shoving the vitamins into us as fast as I can - thank heavens for them!

I saw in a Hong Kong paper that there'd been a heat wave & 41 day drought in the eastern U.S.

Well, more later. I'll be looking forward to mail when we get back to Tel-Aviv.

Love from us both,

X Tinky X

P.S. Just cargo this trip - no passengers - hurray!

We're loaded to 48,000 lbs. - a limit load of spare parts & refuge baggage. We have a new radio operator - Canadian, William Matshewski. Ted Stern left for the States. I gave him your address, & he's going to look you up when he gets to the East Coast.

XX

P.P.S. We're _very_ happy together, dysentery, heat & all!!!!

29 Aug 2006

I finished reading the letter and immediately started commenting on it. I had a lot to move through during this therapy session.

"I wonder if she was paranoid about her health before this trip or if it triggered a lot of her behaviors later in life. She always was a vitamin nut – took tons of them before it became popular. She did love her coffee! It never struck me before reading these letters, but a good cup of coffee was a big thing to her."

"I found a postcard from her:"

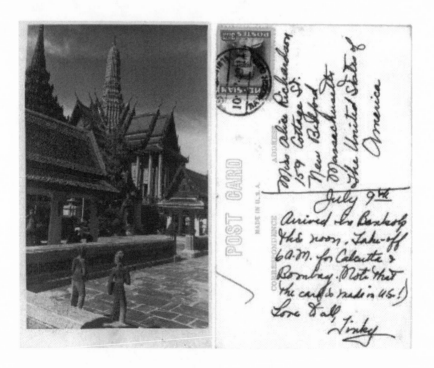

"She loved Bombay! She talked about how beautiful the gardens were there."

I took out another letter.

16 May 1949

CRESCENT HOTEL.

ADEN

May 16th

Dear Folks,

You've never known heat till you've felt it here. The sweat just runs off you! Before we left Asmara yesterday morning, a Mr. Ahronni - one of the leading Jews in Asmara who has financed the flying of many of the refugee loads to Tel-Aviv - took me shopping. They have the loveliest soft, supple leather work in Asmara - sandals, bags & belts in bright colors made by hand by the natives. For a wedding present Mr. Ahronni bought me a red bag & sandals with a matching belt that's being made to order & that he'll ship on, as well as a pair of white sandals with red & blue leatherwork decoration. People are so nice. Mr. & Mrs. Ahronni had us & the rest of the crew to dinner (at 10P.M.) the night before. She can't speak any English.

We got a later start from Asmara than expected - because of our shopping tour - & arrived here around 1P.M. after lunch Herb, Arthur Ford - co-pilot, Mr. & Mrs. Simon & I went shopping for bathing suits for Herb & me since we hadn't brought ours along. Herb got some bright yellow trunks & chose for me a very form-fitting blue latex suit. Then we had a wonderful time shopping for our future home & bought a beautiful and carved chest - the kind that's moth proof & you can store blankets in, and some lovely hand-carved wooden figures. They have beautiful oriental rugs here, but Herb's going to wait on the chance we may someday get to Persia to pick one up.

The Simons, Ford, & us all drove to the beach afterwards. The water was very warm but felt so good we stayed there till dusk. Back here for dinner, then to a Club to meet a friend Herb knows when he was in Ethiopia. We slept on the porch last night, but at 6 A.M. the heat was so stifling we had to come indoors for shelter.

The water supply is very low here - no baths or showers during the day. Leaving sometime this morning. Herb

29 Aug 2006

"Damn – another partial letter! So frustrating...was really interesting. Mom so loved to shop! Even her last year in the nursing home – Deb took her to Filenes in a wheelchair and mom had a ball looking at all the colors and picking up bargains!"

4 Aug 1949

August 4th Thurs eve.

Dear Folks,

The birthday cards arrived today from Beep & Widgie & from Buddy - and I did enjoy them. Tell Buddy I loved his message & I hope his intestines are all straightened out by now & that I miss him very much. During the first month we were married I burst into tears one night & Herb finally got it out of me that I was crying because I missed Buddy - & how I did & still do miss that little fellow. It was nice of Herb to get Mike to keep me company, but tell Buddy he's not half as appealing or affectionate as he & can never take his place. I doubt very much if we will be able to bring him back to the States with us, & I'm having a great deal of trouble feeding him now. He has the biggest appetite I've ever known for a small pup! Also he's being a problem to housebreak, & nice as she is, I don't know how much longer Mrs. Perlman will put up with his piddling. I got up early this morning & scrubbed the floor with a stiff brush to try & remove the traces.

I think of you all so often & wish I could be in the kitchen having breakfast with you or coffee in the afternoon, sitting around the dining-room table. How big that house is going to seem when I get back, & how wonderful it will be. The ties to home are very strong & now & then they give pretty violent twinges. You never get something for nothing.

Herb is still in Aden, & it looks as if he will have to stay there until Maguire can go down & rescue him. By latest reports from New York, Maguire is due here on the 6th. I hope he does come then. I'm reading the biography of John Barrymore "Good Night, Sweet Price", & it is excellent. Also am finally finishing off those argyles I started for Herb, having been unable to get a needle for darning till Mrs. Perlman gave me one.

My love to all & keep writing. It will be a great day when we're together again!

X Tinky X

29 Aug 2006

"Poor mom! How lonely and torn she was. Trying to put on a good front about everything as was her way. I feel very close to her reading this letter. I know this part of her. The one that loved Cottage St; that was tied to New Bedford and her family there. Marrying Dad and flying overseas was probably the bravest thing she ever did. I can see the spectra of returning, finding her mother with terminal cancer, not ever wanting to leave again, and the rift that started between a continuation of a life with Dad and one with her family."

"I found a picture of Dad in Tel-Aviv:"

"He's holding a particularly homely dog. I bet that's Mike. I can see what mom meant. Buddy was an adorable, blond-color, fluffy cocker spaniel. Comparatively, Mike isn't as appealing. It feels so sad when I read about Buddy, knowing that at some point while mom was overseas Grampa put him down."

"I had a start when I read about Mike before I found this picture because we grew up with a dog called Mike, a beagle, who mom had ended up with after the divorce. But obviously that's not the same dog."

---

12 May 1949

May 12th

Yarden Hotel

Dear Mum & Dad,

Herb & Johnny - maintenance man - are in our room working over log sheets. So I'll take this time to catch up on a few letters & have a chat with you. For the past few days we've been having "Kom Seine" - I think that's how it's spelled. That's when the desert winds close in over Tel-Aviv, & boy is it hot & breathless. Then the sea winds come to push them back & the weather returns to normal. There are 50 days of Kom Seine throughout the year. This morning the present spell was broken by rain & now you can breath & it feels heavenly. Yesterday I was hit with the Tel-Aviv blues, starting at 5 A.M. with nausea, cramps & the trots. I ran a slight fever later in the day, only 101.1, but the nausea persisted so Herb got quite anxious & went out for a doctor. He gave me some tablets to take - called "Carbitrene Fortis" - which look & taste like charcoal. They contain Abitrene "Alie"; Bismuth Subnitras; and Carbo Medicinalis. Today I'm much better - on tea & zwiebach with bland diet tomorrow. Seems this is something most people get on their first visit here. The doctor charged $4.50 for his call - not bad, considering the inflation in all else here!

Bob Maguire is due back on the 16ᵗʰ. Whether he's coming on the 54 or planning to go home with us on the 46 we don't know.

I don't know how long our flight home will take. We're stopping in Amsterdam to have the plane overhauled - probably a day in Paris & I know we'll be staying to see Montreal. Usually the planes refuel at Idlewild & go right on to Everett. However, Herb will see if he can arrange it for us to have at least a day in New Bedford to see you.

We've both enjoyed your letters & thanks for writing about the Macy's. I guess the best thing is to sell Holly-Oaks while we can get a good price. Unless Bill wants the things in the museum hadn't you might as well sell them too, if you can? Herb is _very_ much disgusted with his parents' attitude. We started talking *about it this morning & then got laughing so we couldn't stop - that's love for you!*

Be seeing you soon - maybe 7 or 8 days from the time we leave here. The U.S. will look mighty good to us.

Lots of love to all from

Herb & Beth X

---

29 Aug 2006

I carefully folded the letter back up. I was sick of talking about them, about searching for answers I wouldn't find there. I droned on superficially.

"Another letter where she was expecting to leave soon but they apparently didn't. Interesting about Holly-Oaks – I think that was their place down on Martha's Vineyard – part of the cottages on Oak Bluffs. I remember mom talking about the illuminations there and one cottage catching fire from the lanterns. "

"I also have some things that mom said were from 'the museum'. I have no idea what museum that is, but she mentions it again here! Grandpa had some artifacts that were labeled from the museum. I have one of them – it's a stone from some castle!"

"I am glad to have her explanation of Kom Seine – I looked all over the web last time she mentioned it and couldn't find it."

I paused and looked up at my therapist and took a deep breath as instructed, before answering her question to look deeper inside.

"It's interesting – I was telling my sister Deb, how I didn't care to speak to anyone or socialize because when I do it seems so superficial and meaningless. I really don't care what they're saying. I can see their mouths moving but have no interest in what is coming out. She actually feels the same way. I guess that's all part of the mourning process."

"How do I feel? I just would like to feel normal again!"

I felt angry, frustrated, sick of looking at things, sick of being where I was. I heard my therapist's reassuring words that I would be ok. I knew inside she was right.

"Yes I know I will…"

"Do you have Kleenex?"

"Thanks. Ha! Like you wouldn't have Kleenex!"

I blew my nose and then steadied myself.

"I'll be moving on soon, it's near time."

I half wanted confirmation and half wanted my therapist to disagree, but I knew it was the right answer when she agreed. The room looked clearer again. The bookcase came into focus. The ivy plant cascading down its side looked green, shiny and healthy. I looked out the window and noticed the squirrel in the tree outside the window. I looked fondly at the crayons and the stuffed animals. I knew it would all be here if I needed to return but that I could leave it.

"Time's up?"

"OK, thanks…see you Thursday…"

31 Aug 2006

I walked into my therapist's office and sat down heavily. It was time to move on, to get on with my life, to put the letters behind me. I talked quickly to get through all that I had brought. I took the first letter out of the box. I read the letter to my therapist, unwilling to let it out of my hands. There were so few left.

5 August 1949

August 5th

Dear Folks,

I've just come from giving Mike away & though I'm strangely empty without the little fellow around & I know Herb will be disappointed, I had to do it now before I got too attached to him or he to me. Mrs. Perlman had been very patient with his lack of housebreaking until he soaked her couch twice & she stepped in a big move he's done outside her door. He was the "crapingest" pup I ever knew. The floor looked like a cow pasture every morning & I noticed it left a stain on the tiles no matter how much I scrubbed. Besides that, he'd begun to teethe on the chair rungs, & she has some lovely furniture which it would cost a mint to try & replace here. We had to pay damages for the marks he'd left on the floor at ~~Perlman~~ Gordon St. & I could see the bills mounting here. A Great Dane just isn't an apartment pup. So being about at my wits end, especially after he'd yowled all last night & crapped on a sofa cushion, I remembered that Alfred, who ran the bar at the Yarden, had been quite anxious to get one from the same litter. Alfred now has a Café of his own, so feeding Mike would be no problem, a large yard, and two children who were heartbroken over the loss of the big boxer they had & kept begging Alfred to get them another big dog. Alfred is a dog lover of old & former trainer, & Mike will need plenty of training to get him under control before he reaches 190 pounds. So I handed Mike to Alfred & his wife at the Café & they were most appreciative & will give him an excellent home & better care & food than we could. Having some fast growing to do, he ate about twice what Buddy does, & after finishing his own lunch would sit & howl for mine till I had to give it to him to shut him up. That couldn't go on forever.

No ETA from Herb, so I guess he'll wait till Maguire can rescue him. I'd rather have that than have him attempting it back on one engine, but I'll bet it's hotter than blazes in Aden.

Lots of love to all - Buddy,

Beepie & Widgie included -

X Tinky X

I remember I once told you I was through bringing home animals & that sticks! When we have our own home & proper facilities for raising & caring for them - alright - & the same goes for children, though I hope it's not too long before we can come back & settle down to normal living, or as normal as can be obtained with an airlines running your life!

XX

31 Aug 2006

I started spewing stream of conscious thoughts, talking quickly to get it all out as memories flooded into my head:

"Rather ironic that mom gave away Mike and Grandpa put Buddy down."

"Mom was a practical person though. I would have done the same thing too."

"They named their next dog Mike also. He was a small beagle – pure bred. Mom kept him after the divorce, but I think Dad had picked him out. He was a beautiful dog. He had a white tip on his tail and you could see him prancing up the street, happily wagging that white tip, with a corn-cob in his mouth after raiding the neighbor's garbage! He was rather ignored by us kids and I'm not sure if mom liked him or not. Perhaps he brought back too many memories."

"Mike, when he got old, used to pee and crap on papers by the backdoor. It was gross. Then one day he disappeared. I guess mom had to finally have him put to sleep. That must have impacted her on a number of levels. One more connection to Dad gone."

"It's amazing how many childhood memories are brought forward by reading these letters."

I heard my therapist ask what was inside of me.

"I'm seeing such a different side of mom and filling in so many blanks in the sides I did see."

More memories came pouring out:

"I love this letter. It was so mom-like to be bringing animals home so much she had to promise her parents that she'd stop.

She once had 6 cats, all indoor cats! Dad once had 15, but they were indoor/outdoor cats. Even then you couldn't walk without tripping on one of them!"

"Mom was always trying to save the baby birds that the cats brought her as presents. She had about a 50% success rate. You always had to be careful turning on the stove and check first to see if mom had a bird hiding from the cats in there! Her backyards were a cemetery to many dead birds as well as cats who passed away, mainly from old age. And she could coddle them! I left her my cat, Wilton, when I went into the Navy. He was a wonderful cat. She never wanted to give him back so I left him with her. At 18 he had diabetes but she was giving him vitamins and insulin shots and eked another year out of him. All her animals had good lives with her. You can tell how hard it was for her to give away Mike."

"She always wanted children too. That was the only thing that disturbed her about my being gay. She said, 'But dear, don't you want children?' I told her no but that being gay didn't mean I couldn't have them. And I asked her if she had always wanted children. She said that she had. She had wanted two baby dolls that she could dress up and she got two beautiful ones. I think I disappointed her in that dream with my distaste for frilly clothing!"

"But it's a wonderful feeling to have been so wanted. Even if I didn't live up to what she wanted. I was made out of love. Of course she claimed it was a leaky diaphragm that led to my conception... but even so it was an act of love and some active sperms and eggs!"

"And I had two parents, that, with all their idiosyncrasies, I can be proud of in many ways."

There was such a feeling of sadness as I let them go again.

"Thanks for the Kleenex…Can I have the wastebasket too?"

I pulled out another letter. It was different than the rest. I had already read it many times. Dad's handwriting was on the envelope.

"I found this letter in with these others. I wonder why she kept it."

"I never figured out really why they got divorced. I think part of it was that they were so much alike in being impractical. But I also think that it was Dad wanting to further his career, and probably life as a family separate from living with her family, and mom not wanting to play along. This letter sort of implies that as a reason."

---

18 March 1964

Sheraton-Cleveland Hotel Cleveland, Ohio

18 March 64

Dear Beth –

I told Debbie the truth as I see it; which is that we both love her and Heather although we found a divorce necessary. That much assurance she was and is entitled to.

As to the causes of the divorce; I think them now unimportant.

As I told you several years ago I had determined on a path to follow. I have followed it until now with a reasonable degree of success and will continue to follow it.

Be assured I have never spoken of you to the children in any derogatory sense. It is quite bad enough that they should be handicapped to the extent they are. I trust they have the strength to grow up despite their parents.

Herb

"I think that there was this tie that mom had to New Bedford and her family that never allowed her to grow fully into an adult and fly free. Around the time I was born her mother was diagnosed with terminal cancer and died soon after. (Family lore has it that Grandpa mercy killed her.) My great aunt Allie gave up her teaching job to take care of 'the doctor' and his household. It was like a sucking tar pit."

"How do I feel? I feel angry that there were so many secrets."

31 August 2006

"Strange to see Dad's scribbly handwriting in among mom's stuff. For me they were two separate worlds: The world I had with Dad during the monthly visits and later on with Dad & Kit and the family when I moved there, and the world I had with mom, and mom & Deb."

The box was strangely empty. The hollow inside echoed with the past it had held. Only one letter was left inside. I had avoided pulling it out with the rest. It was like turning the last page of an engrossing novel, like leaving a favorite place for the last time, it was losing mom again.

"There's only one letter left in the box. I almost don't want to read it..."

7 August 1949

August 7th Sunday

Dear Mum,

When I went to Amer Lloyd this morning I got your letter telling of your operation, & was

very much upset about it. You poor thing - &
how I wish I could have been home to take
care of you, or at least help out on the domestic end. Call it intuition or wave thoughts - but
I've had the strongest feeling lately that I was
needed at home & even booked passage with
Air-France for the 11ᵗʰ. Herb & I had talked
over my going home to give him a plausible
excuse for getting out of this area. Then, not
knowing how long he'd be delayed in Aden,
& not wanting to leave just as he got back, I
cancelled the reservation. But I think we will
be home before November, keep your fingers
crossed. In the meantime, take care of yourself,
& take it easy, & I'm thinking of you just lots.

No Maguire yet, so I don't know how long
Herb will be in Aden. I'll bet he's melted away
to nothing. Of course it's more than lonesome

here for me, but there are some things you've just got to learn to take & surprisingly enough you find you can! I bought some toweling by the yard & hemmed 4 dishtowels from it, & have also taken the opportunity to finish those argyles for Herb. They look very good.

Ford & his girlfriend come up to see me often, & Nina & I go & sit in one of the Cafés most every evening. I think I mentioned Nina when I first came here. She's Sam Lewis' girlfriend.

I loved your birthday card, & the blouse & stockings sound wonderful. I know we'll be seeing you before too much longer - I just feel it - so till then, loads & loads of love & get better real quick, you mean a lot to me, all my family in New Bedford does -

    XX Tinky XX

31 Aug 2006

I looked up at my therapist, feeling lost, needing grounding.

"That's it. That's the last of the letters. I can't find any more."

I responded to her question:

"I feel frantic. I want to recall all the trash bags we sent to the dump while cleaning out her house and make sure we didn't throw any away! It's far too late for that now though."

A huge feeling of emptiness engulfed me from the inside out.

"I feel so sad and lost!"

I grabbed the Kleenex box and kept it on my lap as if it could help bring me balance.

"I have to let go of her now."

The pain from my chest crawled up through my throat, constricting it, into my head, putting a vice around my forehead and finally spilling out as tears.

"Where's the wastebasket? Thank you..."

I struggled to hold on to the last letter and looked at the final bits to talk about.

"Gagi, that's the nickname we referred to Grandma Perry by, died from cancer a few years after mom returned home – right after I was born. I never heard much about her. Didn't know she had an operation for anything."

"Mom used to talk a lot about intuition and knowing when someone close was sick. She and I had a great bond that way through junior high school. I could forget to make my lunch and silently 'radio' thoughts to her and she'd make me a lunch and bring it to school. Or if I left a book under my bed I'd concentrate really hard and sure enough, she'd crawl under the bed and dig out the book. I was a typical teen so it wasn't like there was only that one book under the bed!"

I sighed and put the letter away. I knew I had to let her go and move on. Her letters had not only shown me another side of her but had been given to me as a gift at a time when I needed it. I would still miss my mother and there were miles of pain and sadness to still walk. But I would move on in my world, enriched by my knowledge of her world, and make it through every day. And I knew that my mother loved me and had tried her best. It was time not only to forgive her, but to also forgive myself.

"I hurt so much inside still. But it's getting better. Thanks to you."

It was time to go. I stood up and walked out the door. But I knew I would return. My journey on my own had just begun.

31 August 2006 – 9pm

Goodbye mom. Travel safely. I hope you're with Dad, your Folks, Allie, and Buddy, and all those you love. And trying on clothing and eating steak by the truck-full!

I do miss you.

Heaps of love,

Heather

XXX

Chapter Three

THE PRESENT

IN LOVING MEMORY
BETH RICHARDSON
MACY
AUG. 9, 1922 — MAY 16, 2006

I wrote this book as part of my own process of moving on after a great loss. In that I found it very therapeutic. In the years since I have become a Licensed Mental Health Counselor and I have found that the death of a parent is a very profound, life altering experience, no matter what the relationship one has to that parent. I have also seen many struggle with trying to find their place in the world, especially after the loss of the last parent (whether that be parent or step-parent). For years I fought my therapist telling me to journal. But I found that writing this over the course of many months was an invaluable tool in my healing and since then have actively journaled during hard times.

In addition to journaling I created a garden in my yard that is "mom's." During tough times and yearly on her birthday I sit and "talk" with her. We all find our ways to cope with loss and move on. That has also helped me.

I do hope that this book helps others as they struggle with their losses in life. As we age there are many. The trick is to go on. My mother used to tell us to "Pull yourself up by your bootstraps." My Dad used to say: "Put your thumb halfway to your nose, your ear to the ground and your nose to the grindstone. And if you can do that, you can do anything."

I also have come far in my understanding of and acceptance of who my mother was. When we are children or still reacting from that child-like state, it is hard to see your parents as just people struggling to get through the world. Some have good tools with which to do that and some do not. My parents were brave, loving and flawed. They were human.

I am proud of the place they held in history, although I'm sure they were not fully aware of it. Dad always used to say; "I took the plane from point A to point B." It didn't matter if there was a forced landing on horrible weather. That's what he did, and that's also what he loved to do.

I daily thank both my parents for the strength they have given me, the genes they have given me, and the sense of adventure and grasping life that I internalized by watching their actions.

Mom and Dad, I still miss you dearly and I know someday I will see you again. Until then rest in peace and know that I have made my peace here on earth.

With much love,

Beth Heather

REFERENCES:

Ahroni, R. (2001), *Jewish Emigration from the Yemen 1951-98.* Carpet Without Magic. SOAS Centre for Near & Middle Eastern Studies, Richmond, UK: Curzon Press

Black, E. (2004), *DISPOSSESSED How Iraq's 2,600-year-old Jewish community was decimated in one decade,* retrieved 28 May 2006, from http://www.bankingonbaghdad.com/archive/ReformJudaism2004V33N2/black.shtml

Flutie54@cs.com, *The Persecution of Jews in Yemen prior to 1948,* retrieved 19 June 2006, from http://www.hsje.org/Jews%20Kicked%20out%20of%20Arab%20Lands%20Part%202.htm

Hahn, P. (2005), *Crisis and Crossfire The United States and the Middle East Since 1945,* Washington, DC., Potomac Books.

McLellan, D., *Robert F. Maguire Jr., 94; pilot called 'Irish Moses',* retrieved 25 May 2006, from http://www.fresh.co.il/vBulletin/showthread.php?t=118498

Meron, Y., *Why Jews Fled the Arab Countries,* retrieved 21 May 2006, from http://www.meforum.org/article/263

Segev, T. (1998), *1949: The First Israelis,* New York: Henry Holt and Company, Inc. Unknown, *American Jewish Joint Distribution Committee,* retrieved 15 June 2006, from http://en.wikipedia.org/wiki/American_Jewish_Joint_Distribution_Committee

Unknown, *Close to the Heart,* retrieved 25 May 2006, from http://www.alaskaair.com/www2/company/History/WootenMagicCarpet.asp

Unknown, *Franklin Delano Roosevelt, Jr.,* retrieved 19 June 2006, from http://en.wikipedia.org/wiki/Franklin_Delano_Roosevelt,_Jr.

Unknown, *Lisa's Nostalgia Cafe,* retrieved 20 May 2006, from http://www.angelfire.com/retro2/lisanostalgia1/40s.html

Unknown, *Magic Carpet Pilots,* retrieved 10 June 2006, from http://www.alaskaair.com/www2/company/History/CarpetPilots.asp

Unknown, *Mediterranean Sea,* retrieved 10 June 2006, from http://www.1911encyclopedia.org/Mediterranean_Sea

Unknown, *Operation Magic Carpet,* retrieved 20 May 2006, from http://www.alaskaair.com/www2/company/History/MagicCarpet.asp

Unknown, Gall Bladder Symptom List, retrieved 10 June 2006, from http://www.skyeherbals.com/pages/gall2.html